What to do
on
THURSDAY

A Layman's Guide to the Practical
Use of the Scriptures

Jay E. Adams

TIMELESS TEXTS
Hackettstown, NJ

To
all those Christians
who really want to learn
how to use their Bibles

CONTENTS

INTRODUCTION

This book grows out of a very real need. In counseling, as well as everywhere else, it is painfully apparent that one major source of difficulty in living for Christ is the nearly universal inability of Christians to use the Bible in a practical way. Scores of counseling problems, and complications added to those problems, might never have arisen had the counselee known how to find biblical solutions to the problems that we face every day. Most Christians seem to have some knowledge of how to study the Bible to glean facts, though even knowledge of this crucial activity is sadly inadequate. Virtually no one, it seems, knows how to discover biblical answers to specific, everyday questions that arise in the course of regular activities at work or at home. Consequently, decisions, often of major proportions, are made regularly without reference to scriptural principles or precepts. And, what is worse, this deficiency is not always due to negligence or lack of concern. Frequently, in great frustration, Christians give up after a number of serious but unsuccessful attempts to discover biblical answers, saying, "I guess that something only an expert can do," or "Maybe Paul could interpret the Scriptures, but I'm not Paul." For them, Christianity becomes academic, abstract and unreal—merely a Sunday affair! Because of courses of action stemming from unbiblical decision-making such persons frequently end up in counseling.

Others, unwilling to allow their faith to dry up, or having gone through just such a dry period, opt for a spirituality that circumvents the Scriptures, finding "answers" to life's problems in experiences, hunches, circumstances, dreams, or even supposed direct revelations. "If the Bible can't be used to produce a joyous, fruitful life, God must have something else for me," they reason. So, whether they realize it or not, they soon find themselves turning from the Scriptures to some subjective, mystical experiential type of modern-day Gnosticism (belief that some "in" group has a special handle on truth and knowledge).

Of course, this "solution" does not satisfy, though for a time it may seem to provide a way that is superior to the lonely, dusty roads of the past because it brings a temporary sense of joy and peace. And it offers answers! But when it wears thin and leads the believer into serious wrong and harm, it leaves the perplexed and battered Christian high and dry, and usually a good bit more cynical than before. Whenever a Christian goes in pursuit of "something else," he is asking for trouble—and he will get it! Yet this is one of the major errors of modern believers that has greatly weakened the church and her witness. It has been the origin of every sort of division, discouragement and heresy. And much of it has been occasioned by inability to use the Bible practically.

It is sad to see such a thing happening in Christ's church, especially since there is no real need for it. The problem cannot be solved by some new, esoteric approach to Christian living that will only tip its hat to the Bible and, therefore, prove a source of error and misdirection. It can be solved by turning back to the Bible in a new way. This time, the Christian must approach the Bible as it was designed to be studied, neither in the tortuous and unfruitful ways that many academics have taught us, nor in the superficial manner that the experience-oriented crowd treats it, but in a careful, practical way that makes it accessible to every believer on Thursday as well as on Sunday.

The truth is that the church has seldom taught the practical use of the Scriptures, and few of the "experts" know how to study the Bible this way. Most seminaries do not teach practical Bible study, and a great deal of what they do teach is calculated to produce an attitude and a methodology in their graduates that perpetuate the opposite. Thus preachers, and those that they teach, end up with little or nothing to help them deal with problems they must face on Thursday.

The Sunday schools and, more recently, Bible study groups that the church has spawned, are not solving the problem. Sunday schools have been devoted largely to the gathering, disseminating and retention of facts, which are filed away neatly for quick retrieval—during the next Bible quiz. Where people have become concerned about the lack of life orientation in these storage-processing activities, they have usually turned to two other equally inadequate and counterproductive approaches: (1) ignorance-and-opinion-pooling discussions and (2) moralizing. Passages of Scripture are ripped out of their context, used as springboards for discourse about one's favorite biases, turned into character studies, typologized out of existence, etc. Interpretation and application of Scripture involving speculation, guessing and moralizing, will continue so long as there is nothing more than intellectual activity at stake. Though they shouldn't, many Christians will put up with that sort of thing for a while. But when it comes to making life decisions ("Should I take this job or that one?" "Is it possible for me to be remarried or not?") they begin to look for something more solid. That's when they realize that lively, speculative discussions will not do. Nor will Bible study guides that consist of little more than a series of booklets with inane and misdirecting questions about the text, with a lot of white space for the student to fill in, do the job. Few, if any of these, teach proper ways to use the Bible. Indeed, to the contrary, they often inculcate wrong methods of Bible study.

Most Christians growing up in Sunday school know the story of Jonah and the whale; or if they've listened closely, they may even know that it was probably a big fish and not a whale. But they wouldn't have the slightest idea about how to use the Book of Jonah on Thursday when faced with a problem or a decision. They just don't think in those terms when studying because they haven't been taught to do so. They have spent time discussing the opinions of liberals about fish swallowing men. (This is all right, but only as an incidental matter.) Thus the Book of Jonah is of practical *use* to them only when engaged in discussions of its authority. And, even then, it is not seen as a book that is directed to them for their everyday life. Its original message, about the need to evangelize and accept repentant enemies when God has forgiven them—no matter how vile and violent they may be—is unknown. Of course, incidentally, one might do well to learn something about how to clear Jonah of false charges and misrepresentations, but not before (or in place of) learning what it is God intended to do to the reader through a study of the book. He should know how to implement its message in his own life before he learns to refute the false statements of others. Somehow, we have put the emphasis on the wrong things. First, he should ask, "How does this book strengthen me, guide me, challenge me, inform me, persuade me?" He should know how he can serve Christ better for having studied the Book of Jonah. He should not let go of the book until it blesses *him*.

Moreover, even in those rare instances where genuine efforts are made to teach the Holy Spirit's intended application of the Scriptures to everyday events, the process most frequently is taught from the wrong perspective. Thought moves exclusively in one direction: from the Scriptures to life. While the ability to move in this direction is essential and always must constitute a fundamental part of every other effort to understand and use the Bible, nevertheless, by itself it remains largely impractical. Problems from Monday to Friday do not arise in the same order as in home Bible study. And decisions about matters not considered in Sunday school during this quarter have a way of demanding immediate attention. They even have the audacity to appear whether or not the pastor has preached on the subject during the past month. The insistent question under which Christians everywhere are laboring (though they do not know how to articulate it) is: "How do I move in the opposite direction?" They want to know how to move from the life situation to the Bible. That is to say, they want to know how to study the Bible in a truly practical manner to meet the contingencies of daily living. They want to know how to go to the Bible to find help on Thursday!

It is just such a use of the Bible that the church has been deficient in teaching. Can it be taught?

If a way of using the Bible on Thursday to meet Thursday's problems cannot be taught, then the Bible cannot be a practical book, and Christians can never learn to live day by day as Christ commanded. Since it is necessary to use the Bible on Thursday, it is possible to teach its Thursday use. It can be taught; indeed, it *must* be taught. And in this book I have tried to teach you.

One reason why the practical use of the Scriptures has not been taught is that it takes much time and original effort to do something that hasn't been done. Another reason is that the persons who ought to be teaching it do not know how to do so. They have been taught to use the Bible in another way, and their natural propensity is to perpetuate what they have learned. Seminaries don't teach it; consequently, pastors don't either. But a third reason is the dangers involved. Abuses are possible. In moving from life to law, from problem to passage, unless one is careful, he may read into the Scriptures what he wants to find there. (Of course, he may do so when moving in the other direction too.) It is possible for him to ask the wrong questions of a passage— questions the passage was never intended to answer—and thus, by perverting the passage, to receive erroneous, inadequate and misleading replies. Again, a person may fasten on one aspect of truth taught in one place and treat it as though it were the whole of the truth that the Bible teaches on the subject, while remaining blissfully, or culpably, ignorant of other passages that sharply qualify or greatly amplify the first passage.[1]

Does *What to do on Thursday* solve all the problems connected with a practical use of the Scriptures? Of course not. To ask the question is to answer it. But it is a beginning; I believe a good beginning. I am convinced that any Christian who learns to skillfully apply the principles and practices taught in this book will discover that he has made a *significant* start, and that by the use of these means the Bible at last has become an important and integral part of everyday living. That is the goal.

While the text was developed as an aid for counselors to use in teaching counselees how to solve problems from the Bible (an essential part of most biblical counseling), the method obviously has much wider application. I see it as especially suitable for new converts, junior high and high school students in Christian schools—they desperately need to be taught the practical use of the Scriptures—and young married couples. But older believers, frustrated with past failures, also may be awakened to make a fresh start at Bible study. And I am convinced that unless seminary students and pastors take up the study of this matter and adopt this or some similar methodology on their own, they will go on replicating for their flocks the crusty, single-direction methods that for so long have been the impractical, unhealthy diet of seminarians. In short, not every Christian needs my book, but everyone needs to do something about the problem.

---

1. For instance, to take the promise of John 16:23, 24 without consideration of other vital qualifications (such as those found in John 15:7; James 4:2, 3; Phil. 4:6, 7) can lead to great disappointment as well as very wrong notions. For more on this see my *More than Redemption* (Phillipsburg, N.J.: Presbyterian and reformed, 1979), pp. 11ff.

PART ONE

BIBLICAL PRACTICALITY

1

THE SCRIPTURES ARE PRACTICAL

For some time I have been encouraging someone to write this book. I have long recognized the need for it both in counseling and in the ordinary life of the church. But, having failed to get someone to design, manufacture and launch the program of practical Bible use that I have in mind, at length I have concluded that I must undertake the task. Otherwise, it appears that the job will not get done.

We have had a spate of books on how to study the Bible recently, but none, so far as I know, with an emphasis on the *practical* use of the Scriptures *from Thursday's perspective.* Most books give information on how to understand the Bible during normal, relaxed study (and that is important and necessary for any other use), but not for its use in emergencies or even in the many day-by-day decisions that one must make before Sunday. They are important for background knowledge, for creating attitudes toward the Bible, and for establishing convictions. And to a small extent I shall find it necessary to overlap that sort of teaching at one point in our study. But the Bible also has to be used at work, in the home, in life situations. How may one prepare himself for such use? His use of the Bible cannot be allocated to relaxed study alone. For many Christians the Bible has become a Sunday book. In *What to do on Thursday,* I shall do my best to help you put your Bible back into your daily weekday life as well; that is my goal.

The method studied here is a direct attempt to teach individuals and groups of individuals how to solve problems biblically. I do not say that it is the only method. My hope is that you will

3

discover that the Scriptures are not impractical, but that we have convinced ourselves that they are by approaching and using them wrongly. The Bible was written to be used in everyday life (cf. II Tim. 3:16).

Bob knows that he must give an answer soon. The proposal has been lying on his desk for over five hours, and his superior wanted a response an hour ago. Bob is a Christian. He isn't sure about the proposal; it may involve shady or unethical practices—but he isn't certain. What does he do? "If only I had a book with answers to problems like this," he mutters. But it doesn't occur to him to turn to the Bible. Once he used to think that the Bible provides such help, but it has been a long time since he has been of that opinion. If you asked him, he'd probably tell you that "the Bible has all the answers to life's problems," but that would be a stock answer to a direct question; it would not be an answer that he would think of implementing at work. For him, the reply would be more theoretical than functional. Practically speaking, beyond the use of some principles generally understood by most Christians, Bob functions on Thursday as though the Bible did not exist. If you were to probe him deeply enough about the inconsistency between his theoretical position and his daily practice, he might say, "Well, I'd like to use the Bible in daily decision making, but I guess I just don't know how. That's probably my fault, but whatever I need to know I can never seem to find in the Bible."

Bob's problem is typical of the distress in which many Christians find themselves because they do not know how to use their Bibles to find answers to perplexing questions that arise during the week. Most of them feel bad about this and would like to do something to rectify the situation, but they don't know what to do.

Bob—and all of those other Bobs who read along with you—let me tell you that there is good news! God *has* given you a practical Book that is designed to help you make everyday decisions. But you will have to work hard to learn how to use that Book properly. Because you have learned too many wrong practices connected with Bible study, it will be more difficult for you; there will be some *unlearning* to do. Success will not come at once. The method has several parts and involves learning a number of skills. But if you don't give up and become discouraged before giving it a fair hearing and adequate effort, you will succeed. Others before you have. Commit yourself to a through effort and you will not be disappointed; less than that will almost certainly guarantee failure.

Paul says this about the practical use of the Scriptures:

> All Scripture is breathed out by God and useful for teaching, for conviction, for correction and for disciplined training in righteousness (II Tim. 3:16).

When Paul declared that the Scriptures (writings in which God has revealed his will to man) are "inspired," he lays the basis for their usefulness: They are not inspired because they are useful, but they are useful because they are inspired.

The word "inspired" has caused some difficulty because it is not a very faithful translation of the original Greek. The English word "inspire" comes from a Latin root meaning "to breath in." The English word, then, is exactly the opposite of the Greek term used by Paul; that term meant "to breath out." *Expired* ("breathed out") would have been a much more accurate rendering, if we could use that term, but it will not do to speak of the expiration of the Bible because of what the English word has come to mean. Moreover, the Greek word is larger. It is a combined word that means, literally, "breathed out by God." As you can see, that is exactly the way that I have translated it in my *Christian Counselor's New Testament*.

To what does this outbreathing by God refer? To speech. One breathes out words when he speaks. What Paul is saying is that God speaks to us by the Scriptures. They are His Word; His speech to man. If you want to hear what God has to say, read the Bible. And the Bible's words are just as much His speech as if you were able to hear Him speak audibly. If you were to hear God speak audibly, He would say nothing more, nothing less, and nothing different from what He has said in the Bible. No wonder then that He calls it useful. It is as useful for daily living as if God Himself were with you, audibly answering your questions day by day.

Because the Scriptures are God's inerrant Word to man, they are useful; therefore, any failure to teach their practical use amounts to keeping God silent. Satan enjoys nothing more than that. And that is just the sorry plight in which so many Christians find themselves most of the time: they act as though they have no word from God.

Paul declares that the Bible has a practical use and then goes on to describe it. The Scriptures are useful to Christians for teaching, for conviction, for correction and for disciplined training in righteousness. These four uses are important.

1. *Teaching*
   The Scriptures teach us all that we need to know about God, man, and the creation to be able to live a life that is pleasing to God. They set the standard for faith (what we must believe) and for practice (what we must do).
2. *Conviction*
   The Spirit uses the Scriptures to convict us of our sins as, in various ways, we fail to measure up to the standards set forth in them. All change from sinful practices to those that please God must begin with conviction of sin.
3. *Correction*
   The Scriptures show us how to repent and find forgiveness of sins and how to begin life afresh. They help us get out of the messes we so often get ourselves into.

4. *Disciplined training in righteousness*
The Scriptures also show us how to stay out of those messes in the future, and they point us to biblical alternatives to our sinful ways. They discipline us in order to make these new ways a habitual part of our everyday living.

All of these uses pertain to the process of change in human living that we call, theologically, sanctification (putting off sinful ways and putting on righteous ones). Just as the Bible has power to bring a person to faith in Christ (a practical use mentioned in v. 15), so too it has the power to help him live more and more in ways that please God. Again, this is a personal, practical matter. Of course, the Bible is the Holy Spirit's Book, and it is He Who empowers those who read it to understand, believe and obey. There is no magic contained in the Book itself.

This practical life orientation of the Bible pervades the pages of the Bible itself. What it says it will do, it does—from Genesis to Revelation. Truth is *never* given for truth's sake alone. It is given to affect life. Listen to these important words:

Paul, a slave of God and an apostle of Jesus Christ to promote the faith of God's chosen people and the full knowledge of the truth that brings about godliness (Titus 1:1).

Paul taught truth *in order to* bring about godliness. So should we study truth for that reason. Paul's purpose, in accordance with the expressed purpose of the Scriptures themselves, was practical. This purpose of bringing about godliness through the Bible is what has either been missed or, in some cases, ineptly and ineffectively pursued.

Nor is the notion of the practicality of the Scriptures of New Testament origin. It is precisely this same practical purpose about which Paul has been speaking that is uppermost in Joshua 1:8 (and elsewhere in the Old Testament):

> This book of the Law must never depart from your
> mouth; you must meditate on it day and night, so
> that you may keep living in accord with all that is
> written in it; for then you will make your way suc-
> cessful, and then you will prosper.

The Bible was for *living* so that one might be successful and prosper in God's ways. And its use was not confined to one day; every day and night it was to be used to guide one in daily living.[1]

If we were to sum up the purpose of the Bible, we would have to say, with Christ, that it is to enable men to love God and to love their neighbors (cf. Matt. 22:37-40). Clearly that is a practical purpose. Everything in the Bible is related to this love-orientation; if love isn't the goal and the outcome (as Paul puts it, "the aim of this authoritative instruction"—I Tim. 1:5), then the whole Bible falls, as does everything else that is suspended on this peg. All too frequently, the law and the prophets have fallen off the peg, not because of any intrinsic failure, but because this preeminently practical end (love) has been supplanted by lifeless, abstract, academic, truth-for-truth's-sake goals and purposes.

The Bible itself consistently maintains that it is a useful book, one that is useful in daily life and ministry. If that is so (and no Christian may deny it), then whenever God's people have found it otherwise, the reason is to be assigned to their inadequate and improper use of the Bible, not to the Bible itself.

From the passages cited above you should take heart: if God says that the Bible is useful for daily living, you can find out how to make it so for yourself. Indeed, if what the Bible says is true, then you may not rest until you discover how to use it practically in your daily life. No lesser goal will do. You must learn

---

1. For help on meditation, see Jay Adams, *Ready to Restore* (Phillipsburg, N.J.: Presbyterian and Reformed Publishing Co., 1981).

how to use the Bible to concretely love God and your neighbor as Christ commands. That is the exciting and profitable task to which you have set yourself in your study of *What to do on Thursday.*

2

A LOOK AT HOW IT WORKS

Let's return to Bob. Let us suppose that the problem he is facing is something like this: Bob has been asked by his superior officer whether he thinks that he would be able to figure out a strategy for implementing a new policy the company is thinking of initiating. Whether it is actually implemented or not will, in large measure, depend on the strategy he develops. Why is Bob having trouble? Not because he lacks ability to implement the change; he is certain that he has the know-how, the ability and even the time. There is no reason whatever for him to plead that he be excused for any of these reasons. No, his hesitation arises from another factor: he suspects—but does not know for sure—that if this proposal is adopted and implemented, the company for which he works may stand to net millions of dollars by what, at first, appears to him to be a change in the quality of a product that will cheat its customers. If his surmises are correct, he will a party to violating the business principle found in Deuteronomy 25:13, 15; Proverbs 11:1; 20:23, and elsewhere, which forbids misrepresentation of quality in business transactions.

Bob might be able to sabotage the contemplated policy by the sort of implementation that he proposes, but his job is to expedite policies by good strategies, not to bottle them up by advancing poor ones. In his mind, there is no question about the policy's basic feasibility, or about how it could be implemented speedily in a simple, efficient and relatively cost-free fashion. He hesitates only because of the morality of the proposal itself; that's his bind.

It is Thursday. The boss has been waiting for an answer. Bob is still uncertain. What shall he do? As a Christian, how does he face the situation? Where does he turn to find the answer?

Now let's suppose that instead of a perplexed, stalled Bob, we are looking over the shoulder of a Bob who knows how to use his Bible on Thursday. His answer will be given to his boss within the five-hour limit. How will he do it? What will his decision be? And how will he make it?

First of all, having reached the dilemma sketched above, Bob will remember and apply the biblical teaching that I have called the "holding principle" (cf. *More than Redemption* for a discussion of this biblical principle). The principle is found in Romans 14:23, which reads:

> But whoever doubts is condemned if he eats, because he doesn't eat in faith; and whatever isn't done in faith is sin.

This principle is broad (note the "whoever" and the "whatever"). It applies to Bob's situation because of Bob's basic uncertainty. He is clearly in "doubt." There is no way that he can proceed "in faith." Bob has investigated the facts as thoroughly as time permits (the principle offers no premium on wilful ignorance). Yet he is still in doubt. The passage, of which he is aware, instructs him (just as clearly as if God were speaking audibly to him), "Don't move ahead on a project that you think may be sin. You must first have those doubts removed." Bob, therefore, may not agree to develop the strategy so long as he thinks that by doing so there is a good possibility that he will be directly participating in a fraud and deception, even if, in fact, there is no cheating of the customer, and his suspicions at length prove wrong. If he had participated while in doubt he would have sinned. He would have done something that he thought might have been sin. In that case Bob's attitude, not the act itself, would have been sinful. To do anything that you suspect might be sin is sin for you, because of your attitude toward God: "I'll do it even though it may be a violation of God's commandments." The holding principle is a very important principle to grasp. In times of doubt it assures us of a proper attitude toward God.

But now let us suppose that Bob has remembered and rightly applied the holding principle; what does he do next? What does the Bible require of him at that point? There are three sorts of passages that come into play:

1. Those that have to do with business and work;
2. Those that have to do with submission and respect for authority;
3. Those that have to do with personal responsibility before God.

Those principles that tell him how to work also tell him to do so "heartily." They tell him to work, not in order to please people, but in order to please Christ (Col. 3:22-25; Eph. 6:5-8). That means that he must be concerned about doing the best job that he can for his employer for Christ's sake. That basic principle requires that he not misrepresent the case by developing a poor, too expensive or otherwise unacceptable strategy when it is in his power to construct a good one. It also requires that in whatever he does, he must serve Christ. If Christ will not allow him to go ahead on the project, then he may not do so—no matter what his employer says. In the end, whether his employer acknowledges it or not, when Bob obeys Christ, he best serves his employer.

Secondly, in all his relationships with his employer he must show the utmost respect, giving honor to whom honor is due. There is an honor due "to all sorts of men" because of their authority, as well as to the "brotherhood", "God", and the "emperor" (I Pet. 2:17). This respectful submission to authority of a business superior is however, the same as submission in any other area: respect is given not to the man because of what he is but to the man *in his office*. That is to say, the Christian respects God's authority wherever he finds it and whoever may possess it—whether it is in the state, the church, the home or the business world. He respects God by doing so. We recognize these authority areas because in the Bible God tells us that He has placed people in places of authority and submission. So, Bob will be respectful to his employer and to any superior officers at work, recognizing that in doing so he is being respectful to God.

But, thirdly, he will remember that God has not given his employer *unrestricted* authority; he has no authority to require Bob to sin. If Bob is asked to break any biblical commandment, he must respectfully refuse, saying in effect, "I must obey God rather than men." That is now Bob's problem. Put simply, it is "Am I asked to sin?" Because Bob knows the holding principle and the business principles that I have surveyed in Colossians and Ephesians, he can move a step further: "I cannot draw up this strategy at this time because I strongly suspect that to do so would make me a party to fraud."

But Bob is only uncertain; he does not yet know all the facts. Thus far, he has not been able to discover them. This means that he is *on hold* and must consider those passages that have to do with one's personal responsibilities before God.

If Bob wants to know what his next step is, he realizes that he must now consider principles like these:

1. "...speaking the truth in love" (Eph. 4:15). The Christian is characterized by this trait; when he knows the truth and must speak, he speaks the truth.
2. "If possible, so far as it depends on you, be at peace with everybody" (Rom. 12:18). He will make every effort

from his side of the relationship to avoid unnecessary arguments and trouble to keep peace.
3. "Love doesn't seek to do anything to harm a neighbor" (Rom. 13:10). He will seek for a solution to the problem that will be beneficial to both his company and to its customers. *Both* are his neighbors.

Obviously, then, Bob must go to his superior and express his misgivings and concerns. He will speak the truth about his dilemma. How he does so will be important. He remembers and looks up a verse to get it exact: "Walk in wisdom before those who are outside, making the most of opportunities. Let your speech at all times be gracious, so that you may know how to answer everyone" (Col. 4:5, 6). He will look on the occasion, then, as an opportunity from God to make the most of it (it didn't just "happen"). And in doing so, he will be very careful not to "Put a stumbling block in anyone's way" (II Cor. 6:3), whether "Jews or Greeks or God's church" (I Cor. 10:32). Indeed, in every biblically legitimate way he will seek to "please all sorts of people in all sorts of matters, not seeking [his] own advantage" but rather the advantage of others (I Cor. 10:33).

That means he will explain his concerns humbly, in careful, wise, well-thought-through language, noting the problems involved: "If I am wondering about this, won't our customers wonder too? What will be our position five years from now if our product breaks down and must be replaced?" If he is able to, he may suggest an alternative: "the problem triggered an idea or two. I wonder what would happen if instead, we...." Throughout, he will keep I Peter 2:12 in mind.

If we were discussing this case in concrete particulars, we could be more explicit about exactly what to say and do, but for now this general, abbreviated description of Bob's thinking and action will have to serve as a guide to point up the general method.

In summarizing what we have seen so far, we note at least the following:

1. The importance of the holding principle.
2. The use of other pertinent principles found in various sorts of passages:
   a. passages having to do with business and work;
   b. passages having to do with authority situations;
   c. passages having to do with personal responsibility:
      (1) those dealing with truth and honesty;
      (2) those dealing with the Christian's relationship to unbelievers.

Other situations will call forth different or additional classes of passages (e.g., passages dealing with the Christian's relationship to believers; passages on forgiveness, reconciliation, church discipline).

The question you may have in mind is this: "How did Bob know about, and go about, locating, understanding, applying and implementing all of these passages?" Some, he already knew. Others, he had to look up and think through. How did he do it? The answers to that question will form a large portion of the rest of this book.

3

WHAT IS INVOLVED?

We have taken a quick look to see what using the Bible is like. Clearly, not all situations will look like Bob's. Nor will the steps in decision making be so apparent; there will be overlap, steps missing, additional steps, and so on. Some decisions will take a longer time. Some will be made much more rapidly (especially about matters that fit into a pattern that has been used often enough for it to be remembered and even to become largely automatic.[1]) Some things are constant. It is these that I shall mention now in a general way.

There are a number of ways to analyze the problem-solving/decision-making situation. For instance, we might see the picture this way.

---

1.   This is one of the goals in the program. What may take longer time at first, soon will be speeded up as the locations, meanings, uses, applications and implications of various scriptural passages become well known. Less and less will one have to look up and study certain passages (though one must be careful; it is easy to deceive one's self when he tries to rely on memory alone and isn't absolutely sure about the content and interpretation of passages). This ability to carry the meaning of biblical passages with you is what the psalmist meant when he wrote, "Your word have I *hidden in my heart* that I might not sin against you" (Ps. 119:11). The Bible must become a part of one's heart (inner life) in order to *use* it in this way. To "hide" in the heart means to "store up" in the heart. The passage refers to more than memorizing verses; it has to do with storing up biblical principles in the heart (the inner life by which one's words and actions are governed). When they are truly stored in the inner life, they will *guide*.

1. A problem arises (or a circumstance calling for decision/action).
2. One must know how to describe or analyze the problem in general terms (evaluate and name it biblically).
3. He must know where in the Bible to locate pertinent principles.
4. He must know how to reach a biblical solution by applying the principles to the situation and laying out a biblical plan for implementing the principles.

On the basis of this format, let's run through a problem situation.

1. A problem arises:
   Another Christian accuses you of trying to undermine his candidacy as a teacher for a Sunday School class. You know that the charge is utterly false. He becomes angry when you tell him so and breaks fellowship with you.
2. A biblical description and analysis of the problem:
   Breaking fellowship is what the Bible calls an unreconciled condition or a "brother having something against you" (Matt. 5:18). In accordance with the instructions found in these passages, you have gone to see him three times in an attempt to become reconciled. But he won't "hear you" (cf. Matt. 18:15ff.). He has told you not to return.
3. Pertinent principles:
   You know that Matthew 18:16 is pertinent.
4. How to reach a biblical solution:
   You also know that Matthew 18:16 sets forth the action to be taken next: you must go to see him, taking one or two others with you. But this plan must be implemented by (1) deciding whom you should take and enlisting their help, (2) setting a time and place for the three of you to make the visit, and (3) deciding which one of you will

ask to make the appointment and lead the discussion (not everyone can do this).

This is a format which (with slight variations on the general theme) might be used in any number of circumstances. Of course, it ought to be used more frequently than it is. That is to say, this general pattern will be followed again and again. Once the biblical pattern has been developed, it will be part of the Christian's repertoire (i.e., stored up in his heart).

Now, let's try a second situation and see how it fits into the paradigm.

1. A problem arises (or in another case, a decision must be made):
   You have found yourself lying again before you realized it, in spite of the fact that you have repented of lying in the past, have had a desire to quit, and have tried to do so.
2. A biblical description and analysis of the problem:
   Your lying is sin; there is no way to excuse it. But it is more than that—it has become a *habitual* problem. You do it automatically when under pressure, and even against your basic desire to stop.
3. Pertinent principles:
   You learn that Ephesians 4:22-25 deals with both lying and putting off habitual lying. "You were taught regarding your previous habit patterns to put off the old person that you were who is corrupted by deceitful desires, being renewed in the spirit of your mind, and to put on the new person that you are who is created in God's likeness with true righteousness. So then, putting off lying, each one must speak truth with his neighbor, since we are members of one another." You also discover from Matthew 5:27-30 the importance of "radical amputation."[1] "You have heard that it was said, 'You shall not commit

adultery.' But I tell you that who ever looks at a woman with the intention of desiring her already has committed adultery with her in his heart. So if your right eye causes you to stumble, tear it out and throw it away from you; it is to your advantage to have one of your members perish than for your whole body to be thrown into Gehenna. And if your right hand causes you to stumble, cut it off and throw it away from you; it is to your advantage to have one of your members perish than for your whole body to go away into Gehenna."

4. How to reach a biblical solution:
   You discover that not only must you repent of the lie and tell the truth to whomever you have misinformed, but you must learn to put on truth-telling as a habitual response to situations in which you now habitually lie. To begin making that change, you will keep a daily record for the next three weeks to discover under what conditions the temptation to lie arises. And you will develop alternative, biblical responses to each tempting circumstance, while prayerfully working at proper responses on a daily basis. That way you will design a complete prevention program to make you aware of tempting situations as they occur and to make it difficult for you to sin again in the same way.

The practical use of the Scriptures, then, involves awareness and a biblical understanding of a problem. A Christian must be able to locate and to interpret Bible passages that throw light on a problem; he also must be able to label and evaluate the problem biblically. (On the importance of correct, biblical labeling, see my book, *The Language of Counseling* [Phillipsburg, N.J.:

---

1. For more on this subject, see my *More than Redemption*, chapter 16. By means of radical amputation, you guard against failure by becoming aware of temptation, structuring against temptation and making it more difficult to succumb to temptation.

Presbyterian and Reformed, 1981]). Second, he must have the capacity to locate, understand and apply to the problem biblical passages that provide the solution to it. Third, he must learn how to lay out plans to implement the biblical solution in concrete ways that grow out of and are consistent at every point with biblical principles.

To put it another way, using the Bible on Thursday to solve problems and make decisions involves:

1. a good knowledge of Bible content, including knowledge of the location of pertinent passages, or knowledge of how to find them;
2. an ability to interpret Scripture, abstracting principles one has found;
3. a knowledge of how to apply scriptural principles to one's situation and how to implement concretely to effect change.

The Christian must continue to grow in these areas of endeavor. Because that is true, I shall now focus in depth on each of these areas of concern separately: Bible information, Bible interpretation, and Bible implementation.

PART TWO

BIBLICAL INFORMATION

4

GETTING TO KNOW YOUR BIBLE

In this chapter, I am not going to urge you to memorize Bible verses. Usually these are memorized out of context and therefore do almost as much harm as good. Over the years we have all heard enough about memorizing. What I have in mind is getting to know where to locate crucial passages of Scripture—for use on Thursday. Our concern will be: *where what is.* A certain number of verses ought to be memorized, of course, but the idea that mere memorization of verses will make one fit to meet life's problems is a fallacy.

One of the major problems among Christians is that apart from Psalm 23, the Lord's prayer, John 3, and I Corinthians 13, there are few widely known locations of specific biblical teachings. (Do you even know where to find the Lord's prayer in the Bible? It's part of the Sermon on the Mount—but where is that?) Many Christians, even after years of Sunday School and church attendance, simply don't know their way around in the Bible. This, then, is the first basic failure that must be corrected.

Many Christians do not know the major thrust (or thrusts) of each book of the Bible. That is where we must begin. Because I have no intention of doing all of the work for you (you will learn better when you have to do some things for yourself), and because I don't want to discourage you by giving you too much all at once, I shall look at the thrusts of the New Testament books alone. Having mastered this material, you may then turn to the Old Testament. When you do, let me suggest that you begin in Proverbs, move next to the Psalms, then take up Genesis and Deuteronomy, and then the rest—in that order.

THE NEW TESTAMENT AS A WHOLE

To begin with, notice that the books of the New Testament fall into four groups:
1. The Gospels
2. Acts
3. The Letters
4. The Revelation

Each of these groups has its own purpose and emphasis:

1. The Gospels are designed to tell us about Christ's ministry (His doings and His teachings) with a special focus on His birth and death. (Note how much space is devoted to the last week of His life.) They are not simply biography: they are selected biography.

2. Acts was written to describe the origin and the growth of the church and its spread from Jerusalem, throughout the Gentile world, to Rome. (Note how it stops abruptly with Paul in Rome.)

3. The Letters were written to churches and to leaders of churches, to deal with questions and problems that had arisen, to encourage them, to teach them what to believe and how to live for Christ.

4. The Book of Revelation constitutes a Christian world view and philosophy of history that predicts events both near and distant, including the downfall of the church's two great enemies, the establishment of the Kingdom of God, and the final consummation of all things.

We might characterize these four sections as:
1. The Man
2. The Movement
3. The Mechanics
4. The Manifestation

You may ask, "Of what practical value is it to know this sort of thing? I thought that you were interested in practical uses of the Scripture." I am. Please be patient; things will come in time. For a glimpse of what practical value the sort of information that

I have given you may have, consider this: Suppose that you are concerned about the "fairness" or "unfairness" of life, and wonder why the righteous suffer and the wicked prosper—then a through study of the martyr passages in the Book of Revelation, together with a look at the interplay of the invisible forces that are at work in human lives and history, should help. The Book of Revelation was designed for practical purposes, not to become the major source of prophetic speculation that it has become. It was designed to encourage, to instruct and to comfort persecuted and suffering saints so that they might overcome (or be victorious over) Satan.

Your concern must always be to discover and to use Scripture for the purposes for which it was given. When Christians don't know where to locate passages applying to problems, they are likely to distort, misinterpret and misapply others that they do know and that seem to apply.

If your problem of decision has to do with some difficulty encountered in everyday living, you will probably want to turn to some pertinent passages in the Letters or, possibly, to some applicable passages in the Gospels (like the Sermon on the Mount) for help. Of course, you will have to know where within each larger unit of the Scriptures to find the particular information that you need. We will come to this later on. But, at the broadest level, when a problem arises on Thursday, your first question ought to be "Hmmmmmmm...let's see now...what parts of the Bible (here, New Testament) are most likely to say something about that?"

THE FOUR GOSPELS

Not only is each of the four Gospels different from the others, but there is a clear division between the first three and the fourth. The first group of Gospels is called the synoptics (meaning those that together view a similar situation similarly). The fourth Gospel, the Gospel of John, has no special name given to it.

The synoptics are alike in that they largely cover the same ground from basically the same perspective. Why should there be three Gospels? There are at least two reasons for this. One is that the law required two or three witnesses to establish a fact. The Gospel writers give witness to the life, ministry, death and resurrection of Christ. The other reason is that, though covering the same ground, there are differences among the three. It is these differences that we shall note next.

Matthew writes as a Jew to Jews. He represents Jesus as the Messiah who fulfilled Old Testament prophecy—note his many quotations from Old Testament prophets. When you understand that, you also understand how the book as a whole, as well as a number of particular parts of it, can be useful in demonstrating that Jesus is the kingly Messiah. Within Matthew's broad sweep—which is chronological—the book selects and groups materials topically.

Mark, in his brief Gospel, portrays Christ as the busy Servant of God (note the repeated use of "immediately") who demonstrates supernatural power over nature, disease, madness and demons.

Luke, "the beloved physician," writes the most complete Gospel, a Gospel that was designed for Gentiles, picturing Christ as full of compassion for the poor and sinful. Unlike Matthew, Luke writes all, even the details, in chronological order, rather than grouping his materials (cf. Luke 1:3).

Knowing each of these emphases will help to orient you generally to the Synoptics. But what about **John**? In his Gospel you meet a theological portrait of Christ, covering a number of different materials and somewhat different ground, principally setting forth Jesus' great signs and speeches to produce a Gospel that features His eternal Deity and saving power. The picture is of God manifest in the flesh; the purpose of the book is to bring readers to a saving faith in Christ (John 20:31). Given this purpose, is there any wonder that so many persons have become Christians through passages of Scripture like John 1:12; 3:16; 3:36; 14:1-5? Here is a clear indication of the point that I am making: When Scripture is used for the purposes for which it is intended, we may expect good results. But to use it correctly, we must first discover the purposes of various books and of their individual parts and sections.

The Gospels, then, are biography with a purpose. The selective biography, and the way in which it is presented in each Gospel, is designed to accomplish the purposes of the author.

THE ACTS

The second division is **Acts.** Luke wrote this book as a sequel to his Gospel. The first treatise (the Gospel), he tells us, was written to describe all that Jesus began to do before His resurrection (Acts 1:1, 2) The Acts contain the continued acts of Jesus (not the acts of the apostles) from heaven by the Holy Spirit through a part of His church. The course of the gospel under those apostles and others who played a significant part in bringing it about is detailed as Luke shows the faith traveling from Jerusalem to Rome. This is a missionary history book, but its thrust is to show that Jesus Christ accomplished His purpose in establishing His church throughout the Mediterranean world during the first generation after His resurrection. It also provides a background for the principal writers of the Letters, for the congregations and the persons to whom they write and for many of the themes to which they address themselves. Throughout, the content of the gospel that was preached (the good news that Christ died a substitutionary death for guilty sinners and that God raised Him from the dead) is continually made clear—cf. 2:23, 24; 3:13-15; 4:10; 5:29-32; 13:28-33; 23:6; 26:33).

THE LETTERS

In the third division there are the letters of Paul and others (Peter, John, James, Jude, and the writer of the letter to the Hebrews). Roughly, this grouping may be divided into two sections:

1. Letters to churches (Romans, I and II Corinthians, Galatians, Ephesians, Philippians, Colossians, I and II Thessalonians, Hebrews, I and II Peter, James, I John, and Jude).

2. Letters to individuals (I and II Timothy, Titus, Philemon, II and III John). Of these, the first three were written to preachers.

From this breakdown, we discover that the letters contain material for churches, for individual members of the church and for leaders.

Romans was written to Christians at Rome, setting forth the need for and plan of salvation (Rom. 1-11) and the implications of this salvation for godly living (Rom. 12-16). Romans 12 contains a discussion of gifts and a powerful section on the believer's relationship to unbelievers (cf. my exposition of this section in *How to Overcome Evil* [Phillipsburg, NJ: Presbyterian and Reformed, 1977]). Romans 13 is the classic passage on the Christian's relationship to the state. Chapter 14 contains a number of important principles on Christian liberty, concluding with the all-important holding principle, which has so much to do with decision making (cf. *More than Redemption*, pp. 31ff.). It is crucial to know where such material is located in each book of the New Testament.

I Corinthians, the letter of church problems, was written to the church at Corinth. It deals with the following subjects: division (chap. 1); wisdom (chap. 2); incest, church discipline (chap. 5); lawsuits and sexual sin (chap. 6); marriage and divorce (chap. 7); Christian liberty (chap. 8); ministerial rights (chap. 9); Christian liberty (chap. 10); the Lord's supper (chap. 11); gifts (chaps. 12, 14); love (chap. 13); the resurrection (chap. 15); Christian giving (chap. 16). If there is a problem in a local church, here is the place to turn first; chances are you will find it discussed here.

II Corinthians concerns the characteristics of an apostolic ministry and is a vindication of Paul's apostleship. Chapter 1 contains basic information about comfort and affliction; chapter 2 deals with the reassimilation of a disciplined church member into the body following repentance; chapter 4 tells how to avoid depression when under great stress; chapter 6 warns against unequal yoking; chapters 8 and 9 have to do with Christian giving, and in 12:12 Paul explains that signs and miracles were given to authenticate apostles. I Corinthians has great chapters and important long sections; II Corinthians has many great verses and significant short sections.

Galatians combats legalism and asserts Christian freedom through a multifaceted argument for justification by faith alone. Like Romans 6-8, chapter 5 speaks of the struggle in the Christian life, the works of the flesh and the Spirit's fruit. In chapter 6 is the mandate for all Christians to counsel (6:1, 2), the rule for paying a minister (6:6), and the overall principle for giving to those in need (6:10).

Ephesians was written to churches in Asia Minor to reveal the eternal plan and purpose of God in salvation (chaps. 1-3) and how it forms the basis for the Christian walk with God and his fellow Christian. In chapter 2 there is a pivotal passage on man's sin by nature and salvation by grace through faith. Chapter 4 regulates the relationships of the members to the body and sets forth solutions to the many problems of communication and anger that tend to divide believers. In chapter 5 there is found a description of the roles of husbands and wives and the basic pattern for dealing with drunkenness and other life-dominating problems. Chapter 6 contains fundamental rules for parent/child and employer/employee relationships. These three relationships treated in chapters 5 and 6 are authority relationships requiring submission and proper use of authority. This is a classic passage on authority relationships.

Philippians was written to give thanks for a gift, to tell about the health, life and work of Epaphroditus, to assure the Philippian church that Paul's imprisonment was not a mistake in which God had erred but was rather a part of His plan to advance the gospel, and to unite the division-torn Philippian church.

Colossians covers much the same material found in Ephesians. But whereas the latter stresses the body, the former stresses the Head. A reference Bible that gives copious cross-references between the two books should be used whenever studying one or the other. The put-off/put-on dynamic of Ephesians 4 is further developed in Colossians 3; and in the same chapter, the Christian work ethic is expanded. The book was written to offset Jewish asceticism and incipient Gnosticism in which the belief that the body was evil militated against the incarnation of Christ.

I Thessalonians is the epistle of hope. In chapter 4 there is an important discussion of sexuality and the acquisition of a wife, as well as the great passage concerning the return of Christ, the resurrection and the translation of believers. Here, as well as in II Thessalonians 3, is an exhortation to work and mind one's own business rather than to develop idle habits that lead to trouble in the church.

II Thessalonians, written to correct errors regarding Christ's second coming, teaches that God will turn the tables on persecutors at that time (chap. 1), warns against false teaching (chap. 2), and again urges diligence rather than idleness.

I Timothy contains detailed instructions about the ministry, including the place of women in the church (chap. 2), the organization and governing of the church (featuring a list of the qualifications for elders and deacons—note the stress is on life, not on gifts and the development of skills), and extensive material on the care of widows (chap. 5).

II Timothy is Paul's last letter. It was written to the man to whom he was about to hand over the torch (chaps. 1, 2), contains directives about the church, urges strict adherence to the Scriptures, especially in times of apostasy (chap. 2), and describes them as "inspired" and "useful" for the evangelization of the lost and the edification and sanctification of believers (chap. 3). This chapter closes by saying that the Bible has all that a pastor needs to pursue the work of the ministry.

Titus was written to instruct Titus in the proper ways to organize and govern churches on the island of Crete. Chapter 1 contains a passage on elders that parallels I Timothy 3. Throughout the book Paul stresses good works among God's people, refers to Christ's manifestation in glory as the blessed hope (2:13), and explains how to discipline divisive persons (3:10). It is a handbook for organizing new churches and for instructing new converts in Christian living.

Philemon is a note from Paul in which he rejoices over the conversion of Onesimus, Philemon's runaway slave. Paul gently pleads for Philemon to release him.

Hebrews, written by an unknown author, who was the companion of an apostle, compares and contrasts the Old and the New Covenants in order to show ostracized Hebrew Christians that what they have in Christ is "better" (the key word of the letter) than what they left behind. The danger of defection is sounded throughout. Chapters 5 and 6 speak of immaturity and Christian growth, chapter 9 speaks of Christ's once-for all sacrifice, and chapter 10 urges mutual ministry among believers and regular attendance at body meetings. Chapter 11 contains the great discourse on faith, chapter 12 has stirring words on discipline, and in chapter 13 there is important teaching on marriage and obedience to elders.

James is a piece of wisdom literature that contains pointed references to the fact that true faith always produces good works. It discusses wisdom, doubt, the tongue, anger, temptation, favoritism, jealousy, judging, unconditional planning, riches, grumbling, and in chapter 5 there is a pivotal discussion of the interrelationships between sickness, prayer, confession and medicine.

I Peter tells us how to endure suffering for Christ. Its message is "trust and obey," doing what pleases God and leaving the outcome to Him. Suffering under an unjust state or an unsaved husband must be endured, and the believer must respect and obey the authority of the one who causes the suffering so long as he or she is not required to sin by doing so. Suffering that issues from a refusal to commit sin must be borne in quiet trust and must not deter one from doing good, even to a persecutor. Directions for elders in chapter 5 are of great importance.

II Peter was written to remind believers of the facts of faith, to warn of coming defection and the advent of false teachers, and to show how they might be identified.

I John is a sequel to John's Gospel. Whereas the Gospel was written to unbelievers to lead them to faith in Christ, I John was written to believers to give them assurance of their salvation. An important section on enabling one to overcome fear by love occurs in chapter 4.

II John was a note written to a Christian woman to encourage her in the faith and to warn against aiding false teachers by giving hospitality to them.

III John is another note concerning hospitality, in which John assures Gaius that he was right in receiving true Christian teachers into his home and promises that he will soon come to deal with Diotrephes, who rejected John's authority and excommunicated any who received the missionaries. Church authority, church discipline—their use and abuse—is an important theme.

Jude is a hurriedly written letter urging its readers to contend against the very false teachers that II Peter had predicted. The difference is that those teachers had now actually appeared on the scene and were making havoc of the church. How to rescue erring Christians from false teachers, while not being caught in their errors, is a subject of practical import (vv. 20-23).

THE REVELATION

The fourth division, like the second, has to do with but one book: Revelation ("the unveiling"). John wrote this book earlier than his letters, sometime before A.D. 70 (the book indicates that the temple was still standing). It tells of God's judgment on apostate Judaism and pagan Rome for their persecution of the church, how God preserves His own, and how He richly blesses those whom He sees fit to be martyred for the faith. At the conclusion it sweeps off into the future, discussing the end of all things, showing the ultimate destiny of all the forces, visible and invisible, that are now at work in human history. It is a book of warning, encouragement, insight, comfort, and instruction that was not intended to satisfy human curiosity or provide material for theological controversy, but to strengthen believers in times of suffering and persecution, to encourage them to endure, and to instruct them to overcome evil to the honor of God.

This rapid survey of the New Testament, of course, is limited in depth. In it I have tried to point out some of the more practical passages having to do with life as we live it on Thursday. But there is much more. Nevertheless, you must begin somewhere. The survey is to acquaint; it is your task to utterly familiarize yourself with every book of the Bible. But, since you must begin somewhere, and because you cannot do everything at once, I offer this truncated look at the New Testament. If you acquire even this much information about the New Testament, it will afford you a firm footing from which to explore the rest. I believe that the selections of materials that you will be learning here will be broad and sufficient to give you a good first year's start. Over the coming year, therefore, I suggest that you learn everything that you have read in the survey. Your first task, then, is to learn this basic minimum. Here is how you can go about the task:

1. **Study and restudy the survey** of the Gospels and the Acts every day for a week.
2. **Repeat to yourself what you have learned**, writing it out on paper and correcting what you have written. You may also want to use flash cards.
3. **Be sure that you learn every location** that is listed and what is at that location. Keep asking yourself, "What is in Matthew 18?" etc.
4. **Skip around, reading in the Gospels and in the Acts** on your own. Note, for instance, how Matthew groups teachings and healings (chaps. 5-9). Note especially how this section is set off by the statement in 4:23 that is repeated in 9:35. Note also the prophetic and judgmental materials grouped in Matthew 23-25.

In Mark, as I said, you will notice the emphasis on what Jesus did, as the busy Servant, not on what He said. Here, we learn more from example than from precept. This Gospel records 19 miracles, while it lists only 4 parables (Matthew has 21 miracles and 15 parables, while John has 20 miracles and 19 discourses).

Study Luke's chronological arrangement:

1. The birth, infancy, and youth of Jesus: 1:1-2:52.
2. The preaching of John, the genealogy of Christ, and His baptism.
3. The ministry of Christ: 4-9:50.
4. The final journey to Jerusalem, the crucifixion, resurrection, and ascension: 9:51-24 (note how many chapters are devoted to this closing period).

Perhaps you'd like to run through the Gospel of John using the following chart:

1:1-1:18	1:9-11	12	13-20		21
		T	13-17	18-20	Epilogue
Prologue	Signs and	R	With the	Death &	
The Word	Speeches	A	Disciples	Resurrection	
----------------	----------------	N	------------------------------		
Revealed	Revelation	S	Revelation		
Rejected	of His glory	I	of His glory		
Received	to the World	T	to His		
		I	Disciples		
		O			
		N			

or, perhaps you would like to note the:

7 SIGNS	7 I AMS	6 FEASTS
water to wine—2	Bread of life—6:35	Passover—2
Noble's son—4	Light of world—8:12; 9:5	Passover—5
Paralytic—5	The door—10:9	Passover—6
Walk on water—6	Good shepherd—10:11	Tabernacles—7
Feeding 5000—6	Resurrection and life—11:25	Dedication—7
Man born blind—9	Way, truth, life—14:6	Passover—12, 13
Raising Lazarus—11	True vine—15:1	

And don't miss the emphasis on the major terms in John: life (36 times), light (22), believe (98), truth (25), world (79), love (36), Jews (71), glory (11).

In Acts, note the outline (1:8) and how the book follows it:
1. The church at Jerusalem: 1:1-8:4
2. The church at Judea and Samaria: 8:5-12
3. The church in the world: 13-28

5. Having done all of this, go on to the rest of the New Testament and do the same three things, taking up half of

the letters the first week, the rest of the letters the second,
and the Revelation on the third.

6. **As you do so,** note especially *where what is*, jot down
key words and passages, draw diagrams, make outlines,
or whatever helps you to remember *what is where*—that
is the important thing to get hold of. It is more important
to memorize *where what is* than to memorize key
verses.[1] Memorize *what* is in chapters and sections. If
you can locate the passages, you can always look up the
verses. You may wish to mark your Bible for quick reference.[2]

Because this emphasis on location—*where to find
what*—has been virtually ignored, many Christians go
through life unable to use their Bibles effectively—especially on Thursday. Read and reread this chapter until
you are thoroughly familiar with it. Read it together with
your Bible, looking up what you read about. Study these
facts until you can state them in your own words. If you
are studying with a group (a very good idea), then quiz
one another on each book, and *where what is* in each,
until *everyone* knows *all* of the information by heart.

---

1. A number of verses should be memorized in context. But beyond that, it is
far more crucial to know what is where. Verses memorized abstractly are
often known and used only out of context.
2. Use one color to mark key verses and another to indicate topics or sections.

5

THE NEXT STEP

When Bob dealt with his problem successfully (chap. 2), you will remember that in addition to referring to the holding principle, he grouped passages from several books. He listed
1. passages that relate to business and work;
2. passages that relate to authority;
3. passages that relate to personal responsibility:
   a. those concerning truth and honesty;
   b. those concerning the Christians relationship to unbelievers.

Here, he was using a principle of theological classification to help him attack his problem. He knew a number of the principal passages on various themes, so that immediately he was able to approach his problem systematically. He may have had to check up on one or two passages that he didn't ordinarily connect with these themes because of the peculiar nature of the circumstances in this case (it is not always possible to work with stock groupings alone), but the topically classified groupings formed the basis for his analysis of the problem (in biblical terms) and for framing a biblical solution to it.

Once one has located various topics on particular themes, it is, therefore, helpful to classify them under general and specific heads, which (incidentally) are not mutually exclusive.

In this chapter, I shall list a number of areas, together with *some* of the principal New Testament passages dealing with each. In addition to those that I have provided (a minimum with which to begin) you may wish to add other Old Testament and New Testament passages in the space that I have left at the end of each topic.

There are many ways to divide life. Bob used one set of categories; here is another:

1. Personal life
2. Family life
3. Work life (includes school and all sorts of non-remunerative work)
4 Social life
5. Church life[1]
6. Civil life

In the list that follows, items are listed alphabetically. After each, in parentheses, is a number (or numbers) from 1 to 6, which identifies it as belonging to a category, or categories, listed above. In using the list, first decide about the major category or categories to which a problem and solution belongs, then check out the various topics numbered as somehow belonging to that category.

NEW TESTAMENT CHECK LIST

Accusation (1,4)
    Luke 3:14
    I Tim 5:19
    I Pet. 3:16
    II Pet. 2:11

Adultery (2,4)
    Matt. 5:28; 15:19; 19:9
    I Cor. 6:9-11
    Heb. 13:4

---

1. Note: God is not in the list; especially is He not confined to category number 5. He must never be identified with any *one* of the categories, or set off from any of them; He is over *all* of them and interested in every one. God is sovereign over all of life.

Age (1)
>   Luke 2:36
>   I Cor. 7:36
>   Titus 2:2,3

Anger (1,4)
>   Matt.5:22
>   Mark 3:5
>   Eph. 4:26-32
>   James 1:19,20

Anxiety (see Worry)

Arrogance (see Pride)

Associations (4,5)
>   Rom.16:17,18
>   I Cor. 5:9-13
>   II Cor. 6:14-18
>   II Tim. 3:5

Assurance (1)
>   Heb. 4:16; 6:11
>   I Pet. 1:3-5
>   II Pet. 1:10
>   I John 5:13,18,19

Avoidance (4,5)
>   I Tim. 6:11
>   II Tim. 2:22

Body (1)
>   Rom. 12:1,2
>   I Cor. 3:16,17; 6:18-20;
>   15
>   II Cor. 5:1-4

Change (1)
>   Matt. 16:24
>   Eph. 4:17-32
>   Col. 3:1-14
>   I Thess. 1:9
>   II Tim. 3:17
>   Heb. 10:25
>   James 1:14,15
>   I Pet. 3:9

Children (see Family)

Church (5)
>   Eph. 4:1-16
>   Heb. 10:25
>   Rev. 2,3

Cleansing (1)
    John 13:10; 15:3
    I Cor. 6:11
    II Cor. 7:1
    James 4:8
    I John 1:7,9

Comfort (1,4)
    Rom. 15:4
    II Cor. 1:4ff.
    I Thess. 4:18

Commandment (1,6)
    Luke 17:3-10
    John 13:34; 15:12
    I Tim. 1:5
    I John 5:2,3

Communication (1,2,3,4,5,6)
    Eph. 4:25-32
    Col. 4:6

Compassion (1,4)
    Mark 1:41
    Luke 10:33; 15:20
    I Pet. 3:8
    I John 3:17

Complaint (1,4)
    John 6:43
    I Cor. 10:10

Confession (1,4)
    James 5:16
    I John 1:9

Conscience (1)
    Mark 6:19
    Acts 24:16
    Rom. 2:15
    I Cor. 8:10,12
    I Tim. 1:5,19; 3:9
    II Tim. 1:3
    Heb. 13:18
    I Pet. 3:16,21

Contention (2,4)
    I Thess. 2:2
    Jude 3

Death (1)
    I Cor. 15:54-58
    Phil. 1:21,23
    Heb. 2:14,15

Conviction (1)
    John 16:7-11
    II Tim. 3:16
    Jude 15

Debt (1,3,4,6)
    Matt. 6:12
    Rom. 13:8
    Philemon 18

Correction (1,5)
    II Tim. 3:16
    Heb. 12:9

Deception (1,4)
    Matt. 24:4
    Rom. 16:17,18
    I Cor. 3:18
    Tit. 1:10
    I John 1:8; 5:7
    II John 2:7
    Rev. 20:3,10

Counsel (1,5)
    Acts 20:31
    Rom. 15:14
    Col. 1:28; 3:16

Decision-making (1)
    II Tim. 3:15-17
    Heb. 11:23-27

Crying (1)
    John 11:35
    Rev. 21:4

Danger (4)
    II Cor. 11:23-28

Denial (1)
    Matt. 10:33; 16:24
    I Tim. 5:8
    II Tim. 2:12,13
    Titus 1:16
    II Pet. 2:1
    I John 2:23

Depression (1)
    II Cor. 4:1-18

Desire (1)
    Matt. 6:21
    Luke 12:31-34
    Rom. 13:14
    Gal. 5:16
    Eph. 2:3
    Titus 2:12; 3:3
    James 1:13-16; 4:2,3
    I Pet. 1:14; 4:2,3
    I John 2:16
    Jude 18

Devil (1)
    Luke 9:1
    Rom. 16:20
    II Cor. 2:11; 11:14; 12:7
    Eph. 4:27; 6:11
    I Tim. 3:7
    II Tim. 2:26
    James 2:7
    I John 3:8
    Rev. 20:10

Discipline (1,2,3,4,5,6)
    I Cor. 5:1-13; 11:29-34
    II Cor. 2:1-11
    Eph. 6:1-4
    I Tim. 4:7
    Heb. 12:7-11

Discouragement (1)
    II Cor. 2:7; 4:8
    Col. 3:21

Division (4,5)
    Matt. 25:32
    Luke 12:49-53
    I Cor. 1:11-13

Divorce (2,5,6)
 Matt. 5:31,32; 19:3-8
 Mark 10:3-5
 I Cor. 7:10-24, 33, 34,
 39, 40

Doubt (1)
 Matt. 21:21
 Rom. 14:23
 James 1:6-8

Drunkenness (1,2,3,4,5,6)
 I Cor. 6:9-11
 Eph. 5:18
 I Pet. 4:3
 Rev. 6:10

Encouragement (1,4,5)
 Acts 11:23
 Rom. 1:12; 15:4,5
 Col. 4:11
 I Thess. 5:11
 Heb. 3:13

Endurance (1)
 Acts 13:43
 Rom. 15:4
 I Cor. 13:7
 II Cor. 1:6
 Heb. 12:2,7
 James 1:12

Enemies (4)
 Matt. 5:44
 Rom. 12:20

Envy (1,4)
 Titus 3:3
 James 3:14-16
 I Pet. 2:1

Error (1,3,5)
 Rom. 1:27
 James 5:20
 I John 4:6

Example (1,2,3,4,5)
    John 15:15
    I Cor. 11:1
    Phil. 4:9
    I Tim. 4:12

Expectation (1)
    Rom. 8:19,23,25
    Gal. 5:5
    I Thess. 1:10
    Titus 2:13

Family (2)
    Husband/Wife
        Eph. 5:22-23
        Col. 3:18-21
        I Pet. 3:1-17
        I Tim. 2:11-15
    Parent/Child
        II Cor. 12:14
        Eph. 6:1-4
        I Tim. 3:4,5

Fear (1,4)
    Matt. 10:26-31
    II Tim. 1:7
    Heb. 2:14,15
    I Pet. 3:6,13,14
    I John 4:18

Forgiveness (4,5)
    Matt. 6:14,15; 18:15-17
    Mark 11:25
    Luke 17:3-10
    Eph. 4:32
    Col. 3:13
    James 5:15
    I John 1:8-10

Friendship (1,4,5)
    John 15:13-15
    James 2:23; 4:4ff.

Fruit (1)
    Matt. 3:8f.; 7:16
    John 12:24; 15:8
    Gal. 5:22ff.

Gifts (1,4,5)
    Rom. 12:3-8
    I Cor. 12-14
    I Pet. 4:10,11

Growth (1)
    Eph. 4:15
    I Pet. 2:2
    II Pet. 3:18

Giving (1,3,4,5)
    Matt. 10:8
    Mark 9:41
    Luke 6:38
    II Cor. 9:7
    James 1:5

Habit (1)
    Rom. 6-7
    Gal. 5:16-21
    Heb. 5:13ff.
    I Pet. 2:14,19

Holding Principle (1)
    Rom. 14:23

Godliness (1)
    I Tim. 2:2; 4:7,8; 6:11
    II Tim. 3:12
    Titus 1:1
    II Pet. 1:3,6

Homosexuality (1,2,3,4,5,6)
    Rom. 1:26-32
    I Cor. 6:9-11
    I Tim. 1:10
    Rev. 22:14

Gossip (1,4)
    James 4:1

Grief (1,2)
    Eph. 4:30
    I Thess. 4:13-18

Hope (1)
    Rom. 8:24; 15:4,5
    Eph. 2:12
    I Thess. 1:3; 4:13-18
    Heb. 6:11,18,19
    I Pet. 1:3
    I John 3:3

Humility (1,4)
    Gal. 6:1,2
    Phil. 2:1-11
    James 4:6,10
    I Pet. 5:6,7

Hypocrisy (1)
    Matt. 6:2,16
    Luke 12:1
    I Pet. 2:1

Idolatry (1)
    I Cor. 10:14
    Gal. 5:20
    Col. 3:5
    I Pet.4:3

Ignorance (1)
    Eph. 4:18
    II Cor 2:11
    II Pet. 3:5

Laziness (1,3)
    Matt. 25:26

Life-dominating Problems
    (1,2,3,4,5,6)
    I Cor. 6:9-12
    Eph. 5:18
    Rev. 21:8; 22:15

Love (1,4)
    Matt. 5:44; 22:39,40
    Rom. 13:10
    I Cor. 13
    I Pet. 1:22
    I John 4:10,19; 5:2,3
    II John 5,6

Lying (1,4)
    Eph. 4:25
    Col. 3:9

Money (1,2,3,4,5,6)
    Matt. 6:24
    Mark 12:17
    I Tim. 6:10

Need (1,3,5)
    Matt. 6:8
    Luke 10:42
    Phil. 4:19
    I Tim. 6:8

Obedience (1,2,3,4,5,6)
    Luke 17:9,10
    Acts 4:19; 5:29
    Eph. 6:1
    Heb. 5:8; 13:17
    I Pet. 1:22

Pain (1)
    Rom. 8:22
    I Cor. 7:8-11
    Rev. 21:4

Peace (1,5,6)
    John 14:27
    Rom. 5:1; 12:18; 14:19
    Phil. 4:6-9
    Col. 3:15
    Heb. 12:14

Persecution (1,4)
    Matt. 5:11,44
    Rom. 12:14
    II Tim. 3:12

Prayer(1)
    Matt. 21:21
    Phil. 4:6
    James 5:15
    I Pet. 4:7

Pride (1,4)
    Mark 7:22
    I Tim. 3:6
    James 4:6
    I John 2:16

Quiet (1,3,4)
    I Thess. 4:11
    I Tim. 2:2
    I Pet. 3:4

Reward/Punishment (4,6)
    II Cor. 2:6; 10:6
    Heb. 10:35; 11:26
    II John 8

Rebuke (4)
    Luke 17:3
    I Tim. 5:1
    II Tim. 4:2
    Titus 1:13

Sexuality (1)
    I Cor. 7:1-5

Sexual Sin (1,2,4)
    Matt. 5:32
    Acts 15:20
    I Cor.5:1; 6:13
    Eph. 5:3
    I Thess. 4:3

Reconciliation (4)
    Matt. 5:23,24; 18:15-17
    Luke 17:3-10

Repentance (1)
    Luke 3:8-14; 24:47
    Acts 3:19; 5:31; 17:30;
        26:20
    II Cor. 7:10; 12:21

Shame (1)
    I Cor.4:14
    I Pet. 3:16

Stealing (1,4,6)
    Eph. 4:28

Resentment (1,4)
    Eph. 4:26
    Heb. 12:15

Suffering (1)
    I Pet. (entire book)

Temptation, Trial (1)
    Matt. 6:13; 26:41
    I Cor. 10:13
    I Tim. 6:9
    James 1:2, 12
    II Pet. 2:9

Work (3)
    I Cor. 15:58
    Col. 3:22-24; 15:58
    I Thess. 4:11
    II Thess. 3:6-15

Vengeance (1, 4, 6)
    Rom. 12:19

Worry (1)
    Matt. 6:24-34
    Phil. 4:6, 7
    I Pet. 5:6, 7

This list is incomplete. It should be supplemented by the use of a concordance and Bible dictionary. But in the list are pivotal passages pertaining to a variety of the more common problems that one faces, categorized for quick reference. Frequent use of this list will help you to familiarize yourself with many New Testament principles and much content.

Another way to use the list is to begin with the six categories and note which topics principally belong to each:

1. Personal
    Accusation
    Adultery
    Age
    Anger
    Assurance
    Body
    Change

    Cleansing
    Comfort
    Commandment
    Communication
    Compassion
    Complaint
    Confession
    Conviction

Correction
Death
Debt
Deception
Decision-making
Denial
Depression
Desire
Devil
Discipline
Discouragement
Doubt
Drunkenness
Encouragement
Endurance
Envy
Error
Example
Expectation
Fear
Friendship
Fruit
Gifts
Giving
Godliness
Gossip
Grief
Growth
Habit
Holding Principle
Homosexuality
Hope
Humility
Hypocrisy

Idolatry
Ignorance
Laziness
Life-dominating Problems
Love
Lying
Money
Need
Obedience
Pain
Peace
Persecution
Prayer
Pride
Quiet
Repentance
Resentment
Sexuality
Sexual Sins
Shame
Stealing
Suffering
Temptation, Trial
Vengeance
Worry

2. **Family**
   Adultery
   Communication
   Discipline
   Divorce
   Drunkenness
   Example
   Family

Grief
Homosexuality
Life-dominating Problems
Money
Obedience
Sexual Sin

3. **Work**
   Communications
   Debt
   Discipline
   Drunkenness
   Error
   Example
   Giving
   Homosexuality
   Laziness
   Life-dominating Problems
   Money
   Need
   Obedience
   Quiet
   Work

4. **Social**
   Accusation
   Adultery
   Anger
   Associations
   Comfort
   Communication
   Compassion
   Complaint
   Confession

Contention
Danger
Debt
Deception
Derision
Discipline
Drunkenness
Encouragement
Enemies
Envy
Example
Fear
Forgiveness
Friendship
Gifts
Giving
Gossip
Homosexuality
Humility
Life-dominating Problems
Love
Lying
Money
Persecution
Pride
Quiet
Rebuke
Reconciliation
Resentment
Reward/Punishment
Sexual Sin
Stealing
Vengeance

5. Church
  Associations
  Avoidance
  Church
  Communication
  Correction
  Discipline
  Division
  Divorce
  Drunkenness
  Encouragement
  Error
  Example
  Forgiveness
  Friendship
  Gifts
  Giving
  Homosexuality
  Life-dominating Problems
  Money

Need
Obedience
Peace

6. Civil
  Commandment
  Communication
  Debt
  Discipline
  Divorce
  Drunkenness
  Homosexuality
  Life-dominating Problems
  Money
  Obedience
  Peace
  Reward/Punishment
  Stealing
  Vengeance

PART THREE

BIBLICAL INTERPRETATION

6

WHAT THEN?

Assuming that you have located the principal passages pertaining to your problem, what do you do then?

The second area in which Christians have difficulty is in Bible interpretation—how to understand the Scriptures.

In this regard, Christians have tended to fail in two ways:

1. They may depend entirely on the writings of others for help.
2. They lean totally on their own unaided understanding.

Neither of these extremes is correct. There must be a proper balance between individual understanding and the help that others can give.

When one depends on the interpretation of others, he must either lean on one or two writers alone or (necessarily) run into great confusion: commentators differ. But if he leans on a selected few, he may never discover that these writers were heavily biased in their interpretations and that much more satisfying understandings of the passages may be obtained from different writers. On the other hand, if he approaches the Bible strictly on his own, disdaining the help of all others, not only will he miss much that he might otherwise have gained, but he will have little or no correction to keep him from wandering far astray, and (at times) even into outright heresy. The Holy Spirit will teach and illuminate the faithful believer, as He has promised, it is true, but we must remember that He does not give His illuminating power to only one person at a time. The Spirit helps others to understand the Scriptures, so that there is the possibility of learning from them what they have learned from Him. Each of us ought to benefit from what He has taught others.

Many of the results of the illuminating work of the Holy Spirit over the years have been recorded cumulatively in commentaries. These aids, and others, should not be avoided. Yet, they are a mixture of human error and correct interpretations, and, unlike the Bible, which is inerrant, must always be evaluated carefully to be sure that they are correct. But before discussing such matters in detail, we must consider another.

Even if Bob is capable of locating principal passages that deal with his problem on Thursday because (1) he has a systematic grasp on a variety of categories of verses, and (2) he knows the locations of many more that may be required beyond those that he has already studied systematically, what does he do on Thursday when a problem arises? Surely it is not always possible to do a detailed Bible study, complete with commentaries and other Bible study aids!

The answer to this is found in Psalm 119:11: "I have treasured Your Word in my heart, so that I won't sin against You." The word "hid," or as it has been translated here, "treasured," has in it the idea of "laying up" or "storing up" treasures. It sometimes also connotes "hiding" or "concealing" something in order to "protect" it. But the important qualifying phrase in this verse is "in my heart."

The principal way to avoid sinning in daily life is to personally possess an abundance of scriptural treasures. Closely allied to Psalm 119:11 is Paul's command in Colossians 3:16, in which internalizing and abundance are emphasized: "Let Christ's Word dwell in you richly,"[1] and the message of Deuteronomy 6:5, 8, 9 (repeated in Deut. 11:18) is:

> These words with which I am now commanding you shall be on your heart.... You shall bind them as a

---

1. The dwelling also indicates a residence in the inner life that amounts to more than the ability to recall to memory; it refers to a *controlling* of the inner life by one who is as much in charge as the head of a household.

token on your hands, wear them on your forehead as a badge, and write them on the doorposts of your houses and on your gates....

Clearly, in all of these passages, God is requiring you to internalize the Scriptures for *use* in day-by-day, Thursday living. According to Deuteronomy 6:5, one loves God with all his heart, soul, and might when he daily lives according to the commandments of God recorded in the Scriptures.

When Moses writes of the Scriptures being "on" the heart, that means more than our phrases "in your heart" or "by heart," which more or less have to do with memorization. The preposition "on" is used in this expression to convey the idea of *affecting* the heart—we might almost translate it "*riding herd on the heart*" (i.e., continually guiding and directing the heart). When the Scriptures lead the inner life (the heart[1]) they will control what one thinks (Scripture on the forehead), does (Scripture on the hand), what goes on in his home (Scripture on the doorpost), and even what he does when he goes out (Scripture on the city gates[2]).

Paul's concept of the "riches" (or treasures) of Christ's Word "dwelling" within says the same thing in a third way. *Dwelling* speaks of a permanent residence within. It is the person *embodying* God's truth; the truth so permeates and influences him that he lives his life out of that treasure or storehouse of truth. Again, the truth is not just there, to be recalled for the next Bible quiz. It is not merely filed for quick retrieval (though that is a part of the process), but it is the dominant influence in daily life.

All of these passages, then, refer to the controlling and guiding power of the Bible.[3] Plainly, God intended the Bible to play a

---

1. For more on the heart, see *More than Redemption*, pp. 113ff.
2. The Jews understood these commands outwardly, missing their true inner significance (cf. Matt. 23:5).

practical part in everyday affairs. But, once again, let me ask your question for you—"How? What does Bob do when he is faced with a problem at work on Thursday?"

I have observed that, even if he wanted to, Bob could not take three or four hours from his work to do a quick Bible study in order to seek an answer. How, then, does he respond?

This problem is precisely the one that is met by the passages that I have been presenting to you in this chapter; they all speak of the Scriptures controlling the life and the decision-making process from their residence *in the heart*. Basically, Bob must know enough Bible—what it says, where it is located (for quick reference), and what it means—to enable him to put together an answer as soon as possible. Usually, when possible, he will refresh his inner understanding by reviewing several portions of the Bible; sometimes, however, he will not be able to do this. So it will be essential for him to know the Bible's teaching on various problems, often *before* the problem arises.

Of course, it is impossible to know everything. Knowledge grows in depth and breadth over time. There are many questions that do take time to research for answers; and there are often two or three days available for doing such research prior to action. So, not all decisions must be made on the run. Indeed, many Christians make decisions too quickly. When a decision or action may be postponed, it is often desirable to postpone it so that there will be time to do biblical research or to check up biblically on the first response that comes to mind. Each time that adequate research is done, the one doing it is in a better position than ever before to make quick decisions in the future. He can rely on past work for future reference.

"But," you ask somewhat insistently, "How can I get enough information quickly enough to know what to do on Thursday?" Well, if you have a genuine desire to please God,

---

3. On guidance by the Scriptures alone, see *More than Redemption*, pp. 23ff.

you will want to discern as much of His will as you can. You will faithfully be storing up Scripture, properly interpreted and related to other passages of Scripture, every day. You will not wait until the problem comes to go running for your Bible. The more that you learn through daily study and thoughtful, meditative assimilation of the truth into life, the more prepared you will be to meet it when the crunch comes on Thursday. And the more that you learn on Monday, Sunday, Friday, etc., the more often you will find yourself able to respond quickly on Thursday. Don't be concerned about how much or how little knowledge you have at the moment; just continually get all that you can. God is in charge of this world; nothing takes place that shouldn't. Everything happens at the right time. Therefore, God will bring into your life exactly what you can handle at any given time, if you handle it His way, according to the Scripture that you do know, asking the Spirit to strengthen you (cf. I Cor. 10:13).[1] Don't think that you cannot begin to use the Scriptures in daily life until you have mastered some arbitrary minimum number of passages. How much Bible is "enough" Bible for a person to know? You will find that if you think that way you will never begin, because you will soon learn that you can never have "enough" of God's Word. No, you must begin prayerfully where you are, with what you have.

In the meantime, soberly assessing your strengths and weaknesses, you must make every attempt to learn what you do not know. Indeed, after every failure—and there will be failures—you must go home and mend your net. Failures ought to spur you on to repentance and further study, not lead you into discouragement. You must go back to the Scriptures and study Them until you know *for sure* what you must know to avoid the failure in the future. But you ought not to depend on failure

---

1. But now and then, expect God to throw you a curve when you become complacent or cocksure in your attitudes about your knowledge or life in order to drive you back to the Scriptures in humble repentance.

alone as a motive to learn. You must "store up" God's Word in your heart so that—in the future, when the problem comes—you might not sin against Him. Most of your study, therefore, should be preventive, not remedial.

So Bob, and you, regularly must take time to locate, study, and learn the meaning of more and more portions of the Bible, categorizing them (perhaps as I have in the previous chapter) for ready reference when problems and decisions arise in days to come.

But where does one begin? Although it is by no means adequate, the list of passages in the previous chapter provides a convenient starting place. Here is my practical suggestion for preparing you to use that list.

1. Make a quick survey of all of the passages listed. Read them all.
2. As you read them in a modern translation (such as *The Christian Counselor's New Testament* [Timeless Texts, 1995]), put a check mark next to every passage that you can locate with no difficulty.
3. Put a second check next to those which you are sure you know the meaning of (don't fool yourself; be sure or don't check it).
4. Put a third check next to those which you either have implemented in previous problem-situations or decisions, or believe that you could implement properly.
5. Then, over a period of time, regularly study those passages with no check, one check or two checks.
6. As you learn more and more about these passages, continue to check them off until you have a triple check mark next to every passage on the list.
7. After that:
   a. Review regularly.
   b. Add other New Testament and Old Testament passages to your list.

    c. Repeat the study process until you have triple checks beside all of these additional passages too.

"OK, that sounds like a workable plan. I can see some wisdom in it and I would like to begin. But how do I go about studying a passage in order to understand its meaning? If you don't tell me that, I may forever be trying to make my first check marks!" The answer to that good question is the concern of the next chapter.

7

INTERPRETING THE WORDS
OF SCRIPTURE

There are three fundamental activities involved in the process of
Bible interpretation:
1. Interpreting the words
2. Interpreting the passage
3. Interpreting the purpose
There are other ways of expressing the ideas behind these three
activities, but the way that I have described them seems clearest
for the present book.

Each of these three activities, in turn, involves certain concerns. Here we shall look closely at how to interpret the words of
Scripture.

In order to interpret a portion of the Bible, you must understand the words that are used in the passage under consideration.
Moreover, you must understand them individually and in relationship to each other. That means that you must know something of the vocabulary, the grammar, and the syntax of a
passage.

The last sentence that you just read contains the words
"grammar" and "syntax." And this entire section of the book
contains the word "interpret." I'd be kidding myself, and at the
same time possibly would be allowing you to do the same, if I
didn't take the time to discuss those three words briefly. The
same sort of discussion is needed, let me point out, when
attempting to interpret biblical terms.

Often, however, we wrongly assume that we know what
such words mean as we read them, when all that we really have

is a fuzzy or inaccurate understanding of them. Take the word "interpret," for instance. How do you interpret that word? Using it in a sentence that way, in this context, already begins to make clear (i.e., interpret) to you something of its meaning. That is because context helps you to interpret. The English word means "to make the meaning of something clear." The Greek word for interpretation, found in John 1:18, Luke 24:35, an Acts 21:19, literally means "to lead out." The idea behind this "leading out" is to "show one the way" something really is. You are leading one out to see it as, in fact, it is.

Now how could you, on your own, reach any such understanding of a biblical word if you wanted to interpret a passage? You know that you can learn the meaning of an English word from a dictionary. But how do you learn about a Greek word in the New Testament? The same way; you use a Greek dictionary. "But I don't know Greek," you object. I know that. But you don't have to know Greek in order to do simple word studies. Instead, you should buy, *and use*, a copy of W. E. Vine's *An Expository Dictionary of the New Testament Words for English Readers* (Fleming H. Revell Co., 1966). On all counts, this is the most comprehensive and useful volume available for the serious student of the New Testament who doesn't read Greek. Everything, even the transliteration of Greek words themselves, is in English (transliteration means writing Greek words in the letters of the English alphabet).

By the word "grammar" I refer to the forms of words and their arrangement into sentences; by syntax, I mean the relationship of words and sentences to one another. So, biblical interpretation (showing someone else what a passage of Scripture, or some portion of it, means) involves study of words and sentences. It is a matter, first of all, of what the words and sentences mean.

Such study requires a study of vocabulary. That is where Vine comes in handy. But, as the advent of numerous translations makes abundantly clear, there is not always agreement on the translation of a word, and there is more than one meaning to many words. Looking up the use of a term in Vine will also help to emphasize the point; often, he will give you a number of meanings, frequently telling you how it ought to be translated in a given passage. But, while Vine is very helpful and generally trustworthy, you will not be able to follow him without question on every opinion. That is why you will need more than Vine (but if you can afford only one such book at the outset, get Vine).

If there are various possible meanings to a word, how does one know which is the best meaning in a particular passage? Let me suggest four ways of helping you reach a decision:

1. **Context**, as I have noted, often will give you the clue. Take the words "test" and "tempt." In the Greek there is but one word for both ideas. Clearly, when the Bible says that God "tested" Abraham, that is the word that best describes what God did. The King James Version confuses the matter by translating it "tempt." This is clear because, according to James 1:13ff., God "tempts no one" (and, contextually, again we know that is how the same word ought to be translated in James). Every situation is both a test and a temptation, depending on whose viewpoint of it you are considering: God tests to strengthen; Satan tempts to weaken.

2. **Similar usage**, either by the same author (who may always use a word in a particular way), or use of the word in a similar context by some other writer, provides an excellent help. "Soul" has several biblical meanings. But in the Psalms, again and again, it is used poetically to mean "self" and "myself." So, in poetic study, one will be alert to such a possibility. For comparative studies, a good cross-reference Bible and a complete concordance (Monser's *Cross Reference Bible* and Strong's *Concordance* would be the best for you) will be found essential.

3. **Commentaries** are so important that I shall have to say more about them at a later point. But, for now, let me observe

that while commentaries differ, often they will agree—especially on word usage. Thus, in addition to all the rest of the help that they afford, they become an important source of information in word study. But always use more than one (never fewer than three) to be sure that there is no significant difference of opinion. When they differ, you will have to make up your mind for yourself which, if any of them, is correct. You will do this by evaluating the arguments that they put forth for their positions, and by following the guidelines that I have already given.

4. **Translations** provide the easiest way to compare opinions of word usage. Because of this, they are the first place to begin. Every serious Bible student should have several translations on his study shelf; and soon each should be well worn. I would suggest that you get at least five complete translations of the entire Bible and at least three more New Testament translations. Here are my suggestions:

a. **Complete Bible:** New King James Version, Revised Version of 1881 (or American Standard Version of 1901), New American Standard, Berkeley, New International Version.

b. **New Testament only:** *The New Testament in Everyday English* (this is the text used in *The Christian Counselor's New Testament*, which I have quoted throughout this book), Williams, Revised Standard Version (New Testament only).

Because it is not a translation, but a paraphrase, *The Living Bible* is omitted from the list. The best place on the shelf to put it is among your commentaries because it is not a translation but one man's opinion on the meanings of various passages.

Immediately, by consulting translations, you can tell whether there is a general consensus on the meaning of a word or whether there is wide difference of opinion. You can more or less tell what sort of work is cut out for you. If all agree, then you can often (not always) bypass detailed word study; if they disagree, you know you will have to settle down to some hard work. Get out Vine and your commentaries.

Much more could be said about interpreting words, but these four guidelines will prove most helpful, and those who follow them closely will discover that doing so will lead to other helps (mentioned in commentaries, etc.), which will further enhance your understanding.

Word study is important, more important than many people think, and every interpreter of the Scripture must become familiar with a procedure (mine or some other[1]) for getting at the meaning of words.

At this point, let us take an example or two to see how word study throws light on a text. Let us consider the words "renew" and "spirit" as they are used in Ephesians 4:23. All versions use "renew" as the translation of *ananeoo.* So it *looks* as though there will be little reason for the study of the word. Yet previous study of the term "new" has led you to realize that there are two words in the original Greek New Testament translated by the one English word "new" (*kainos,* meaning "brand new," and *neos,* meaning "young" or "new to you"). You are curious to see if there is more than one word translated "renew." So you look up the words in Strong's concordance and find that, sure enough, there are two. Here, the word, you find out from various sources, means to "make young" or "youthful," not merely to "make different" or to "make fresh" as *anakainoo* does in II Corinthians 4:16 and Colossians 3:10.

A study of the commentators, Vine, and translations also helps you to understand the word "spirit." For instance, Berkeley and the NIV, with their translations "mental attitude" and "attitude of mind," clue you in on the fact that spirit here does not refer to the Holy Spirit, but to the human attitude (though you find that some commentators disagree). While Vine gives a variety of meanings for "spirit," he neglects altogether the one that you adopt. You conclude, rightly, that Vine is not infallible (nor

---

1. Greek scholars, of course, will have a number of other helps available to them.

is the Berkeley, nor the NIV translators that you follow in this case because they seem to be right).

The translators and commentators point out (and here Vine agrees) that the change viewed is not in the mind itself, but in the spirit (attitude) that the mind takes toward God's new ways. So, there is a renewal of mental attitude.

Now, putting it all together, you come out with this: there must be a rejuvenation (renewal by making youthful) of one's mental attitude toward God's Word that will enable him to put off old ways and put on new ones. This pictures for us the sort of attitude that Adam originally must have had toward all of God's creation and God's ways before the fall. It was a youthful, anxious-to-learn and anxious-to-please attitude that is restored in the believer by regeneration. This word study throws light on a passage that is otherwise darkened by habitually insipid translations.

It is also important to recognize that the same word may have several meanings. In Isaiah 45:7 we read, "I form the light and create darkness; I make peace and create evil." The Hebrew word translated "evil" means both moral offense ("sin") and calamity. Here, the phrase itself, along with the parallelism in the verse, makes the choice between the two meanings for us. The evil in the passage is "trouble" or "calamity," since it must be the opposite of *peace*, just as darkness is the opposite of *light*. Here, an understanding of rhetorical form enables us to interpret correctly.

Grammatical interpretation is also of great importance. When reading I Peter 3:1, for instance, the King James Version says that an unsaved husband (one who disobeys the Word) may be won "without the word." How can that be in the light of Romans 10:17 ("Faith comes by hearing, and hearing by the word")? As translated, the two verses stand in contradiction to one another. But in the original Greek there is no contradiction at all. Better translations of the passage, and commentaries, will point out that the original reads "without a word," not "without the word." That makes all of the difference in the world! It is the wife's word (not God's) that is in view. She is not to preach to or nag her husband with the gospel.

The procedures that I have outlined here are simple but take time and effort. Yet, followed faithfully, they will give you a fruitful working method for understanding vocabulary, grammar and syntax.

In the next chapter, I shall look at the importance of interpreting the passage as a whole. Before doing so, however, let me say a word about commentaries, since they have figured so largely in my discussion of interpretation thus far.

MORE ABOUT COMMENTARIES

There are several types of commentaries:

1. **One-volume commentaries**—best for a quick survey, for understanding the flow of an argument or passage, but not as good for grammatical and word study. I recommend the *New Bible Commentary* published by Eerdmans.

2. **Commentary sets**—these are by one author or several. Among the best are *Calvin's Commentaries* (Baker), *Lange's Commentary* (Zondervan), *The New International Commentary on the New Testament* (Eerdmans), *The New Testament Commentary* by Hendriksen (Baker), *The Tyndale New Testament Commentary* (Eerdmans) and *The Christian Counselor's Commentaries on the New Testament* by Adams (Timeless Texts).

3. **Commentaries on individual books of the Bible**— Often these are the best. Here there are too many commentaries to mention. The best thing to do is to ask your pastor or some other knowledgeable Christian for advice. Try to look through his library and see the books before purchasing them for yourself. You can also look through books at a local Christian bookstore.

Final note: For word studies, Vincent's *Word Studies* and A. T. Robertson's *Word Pictures* are an excellent supplement to Vine.

8

INTERPRETING THE PASSAGE

In this chapter, I am more concerned about the historical, cultural, rhetorical and theological understanding of a passage than its grammatical meaning. In order to do this kind of study, again you should invest in some books that will help.

First, let me suggest that a good Bible dictionary will be an invaluable aid. I recommend *The New Bible Dictionary* (Eerdmans) and ISBE (*The International Standard Bible Encyclopedia*), a comprehensive, five volume set (Eerdmans). In these books you will find a wealth of historical, archeological, cultural, factual, geographical and other sorts of background information that are invaluable to an understanding of any number of biblical passages. H. H. Haley's *Pocket Bible Handbook* is a good supplement to your Bible dictionary. In addition, a book or two on theology would be helpful. I suggest L. Berkhof's *Manual* or his *Systematic Theology* (the latter is larger), A. A. Hodge's *Outlines of Theology*, and, in a more practical vein, my *More than Redemption* (the first two are published by Eerdmans and the last by Zondervan). Careful use of these volumes will help you understand the meaning and interrelationship of passages as you study your Bible.

HISTORICAL INTERPRETATION

The study of history is vital, for instance, to an interpretation of the latter chapters of the Book of Daniel (e.g., to relate chapters 11 and 12 to the history of Antiochus Epiphanes), and to much of the Book of Revelation (here the history of Rome is helpful), just to mention two. But it becomes important in many individual passages as well. For instance, the history of the destruction of Jerusalem, as it is recorded in Josephus' history (this record in turn is often quoted and summarized in other places such as in Bible dictionaries), is important to an understanding of the Olivet Discourse in Matthew 24, Luke 21, and Mark 13. Many of the Old Testament passages have to do with nations from the historical past that no longer exist. To fully understand some of the historical allusions made in the Bible, it is helpful to know something of them and of their history.

I have mentioned the book of Jonah. Let's look at it again. The people to whom that book was written knew much about Nineveh, that great and wicked city (Jonah 1:1). You probably don't. When they were reminded of its "wickedness" therefore, all sorts of events, well known to them, flashed into their minds. They do not flash into yours. So, the use of a Bible dictionary would help (as well as a good commentary).

What would you find as you researched material on Nineveh, Assyria and Jonah? You would get all sorts of information, including something about the city's enormous size, and of the atrocities and cruelties performed by it's inhabitants upon their enemies. You would understand better what the wickedness of the city was like when you learned that they skinned enemies alive, cut off hands, feet, ears and noses, put out eyes and pulled out tongues. You would learn that the city of Nineveh had streets lined with the skulls of persons from conquered nations, and that it was this kind of city that was threatening to destroy Jonah's own people. Jonah's reluctance, seen in the light of these facts, cannot be dismissed as merely some kind of Jewish prejudice or narrow nationalism; it must be seen as a deep resentment toward Nineveh. That is why God speaks of Jonah's "anger" (4:1, 9, 11). It was a bitter hatred that motivated Jonah to go the other way and that made him angry over the fact that God did not destroy Nineveh. He wanted to see the Ninevites punished for their crimes. He had no mercy. Knowing these facts helps us to understand why Jonah acted as he did about this "bloody city." History and archeology, therefore, can be very helpful.

CULTURAL INTERPRETATION

When we read of persons going up on the housetops and digging through roofs, it is useful to know something of the design of houses and the customs of persons that were common in Palestine at that time. Roofs were flat, often made of logs and mud. People spent much time on them, and even slept on them on hot nights. They went to the roof to meditate and to pray. Usually, there was a stair on the outside of the house that led to the roof. You can learn all this and everything else that you need to know about roofs from Bible dictionaries. There are many references to roofs in the Bible, and some knowledge of houses and customs connected with them is of value in understanding those references.

Take another example: In Matthew 16:18, Christ speaks of the "gates of hades," and in Proverbs 31:23, we read of the virtuous women's husband sitting "in the gates." What on earth does that mean? A good Bible dictionary will make it clear that the gate of an ancient Near Eastern city was not a wooden door on hinges, but a room in which the town elders met to hold counsel. To "sit in the gate" is to sit *as an elder or ruler of the city.* To say that the gates of hades (another word to look up) "will not prevail" against the church is to declare that all the counsels of those evil powers in the unseen world (you will find that hades means the "unseen world") against the church will fail.

To know something of the coinage of Christ's day is of importance in interpreting His words in Mark 12:17. In a talk, "The Church and Her Rights," published in a pamphlet form by the same name,[1] I made interpretive use of such knowledge. Among other things I wrote:

---

1.   Obtainable from CCEF, 1790 E. Willow Grove Ave., Laverock, PA 19118.

It came like an electric shock to the Pharisees and the Herodians! Their representatives had cautiously concealed their true motives. They had carefully buttered Him up. Their question was a valid and vital one that He could avoid answering only at the cost of injuring His reputation. And...whichever answer He gave, He was sure to lose. If He said yes, the Hebrew patriots would turn against Him; if He said no, He would imperil His relationship to the Roman government. The trap seemed perfect; there was no escape. But *that* answer—wholly unsuspected and entirely satisfactory, pinned them to the wall by the ears. No wonder, as Mark put it, "they were astounded" (v. 17).

But was Christ's reply merely a clever retort, designed to avoid both horns of a dilemma while stopping the mouths of hypocritical flatters? Clearly, it was *that*. But was there more? At the same time, did Jesus teach us something vital about the relationship of church and state?

Yes. His words are not a calculated enigma. Far from it! What they are is a profound and far-reaching statement of the principle by which the church in any situation may evaluate its relationship to the state. But what is the principle; what was He saying? And what (if anything) does it have to do with the problem that has brought us together tonight?

The silver coin—the Roman denarius that Jesus requested—provides the clue we need to rightly interpret His words; the whole story is on the coin.

The "Caesar" to whom Jesus referred was Tiberius, whose image and inscription were on that small silver coin that was worth a day's wages. The hated poll tax over which the discussion arose was due once a year, cost one denarius per adult, and had to be paid in this coin alone.

Now, in coming to an understanding of Christ's principle, it is vital to note that Jesus directed attention to the coin itself. He pointed both to the head of Tiberius and to the words engraved on the coin. On the *obverse*, around the head, was written:

"Tiberius Caesar Augustus, son of the divine Augustus."

On the *reverse* was a picture of Tiberius' mother, Livia, represented as the goddess PAX ("peace") together with the words *Pontif Maxim* ("highest priest"). Now, what did Jesus want us to see in all of that?

First, Jesus was saying "Pay the tax. God has given Tiberius the right to raise funds to pay for the army, the police protection, the Roman roads, and the courts that he has provided for you. This money belongs to him as plainly as the coin is his." That much is clear, and is the consistent teaching of the entire New Testament. But then He said, "Pay to God what belongs to Him."' What did He mean by that? What *else* did He see on the coin?

The denarius contained blasphemous words—calling the former emperor divine, designating Tiberius as God's high priest, and representing his mother as a pagan goddess. These unmistakably religious claims, though mixed with true ones, were false and unacceptable. Such belief and worship as they implied were due to Jehovah and to Him alone.

Jesus, the true High Priest, would not share His honor with another—not even with the emperor of Rome.

So, to begin with, He was saying, "Give Caesar his taxes, but don't give him the worship that he desires; give that to God alone." Fundamentally, that is the principle: all of Caesar's claims must be examined; only those that belong to him may be met.

But, now secondly, we see that although God has granted authority to the state, that authority is *not* unlimited. Caesar has rights, but God has reserved rights for Himself. The sovereign authority that belongs to God alone must not be usurped by any human political ruler. Caesar's authority extends only so far as the Bible permits him to go and no further. And because He has granted it, God is sovereign even over that authority which He granted. (In John 19:11, Jesus told Pilate, "You wouldn't have any authority over me if it hadn't been given to you from above.")

Thirdly, notice how Caesar, in addition to temporal rule, was claiming rights to a spiritual kingdom and spiritual authority over the very consciences of his subjects. Christ's words plainly warn us that there are *two* realms, *two* rulers over us, *two* authorities with whom we have to do—not one. One has sway on earth over a temporal kingdom; the other reigns from heaven over a kingdom that is *in*, but not of, this world (John 18:36). In every decision, therefore, the church must determine whether compliance with the state means noncompliance with God. Christ's words make it clear that one must comply with the demands of the state, but only so far as the state's requirements remain within the bounds of the legitimate authority that God has given to it. When the state also attempts to order the internal affairs of Christ's kingdom (the church) a conflict arises, in which, as the apostles later put it, "We must obey God rather than men" (Acts 5:29).

All true authority is from God—authority in the home, in the church and in the state, therefore, he obeys God. So then, there can be no conflict in the exercise of authority in these realms when it is exercised according to the biblical limits prescribed for each. Problems arise when those in either one or more areas overreach their limits. At that point the transgressor of God's boundaries no longer speaks with the authority of God, but merely as a human being.

Notice, in the apostles' words there is no pitting of God's authority given to the state against God's authority given to the church—what they indicate is *exactly not* that. That could be; God does not contradict Himself. No, as they say, "We must obey *God* rather than *men*." The state, in transgressing biblical boundaries had begun to exercise a purely human authority that was not given by God and was, in fact, in opposition to God. It is possible, of course, for the home or for the church also to overstep God's boundaries circumscribed in the Scriptures. But early in her history the church was faced with state expansionism, a tendency on the part of the state that she has often had to grapple with ever since. Caesar's greatest temptation is to claim rights to that which belongs to God above. The course that the church must take was charted originally by Christ in

His words regarding God and Caesar and early followed by the apostles who provided her with an example for all time. God must be given what is His; when the state says no, the church must obey God rather than man. To put it simply, whenever a state requires a Christian to sin—i.e., to disobey God—he must refuse.

RHETORICAL INTERPRETATION

There are many different kinds of literature in the Bible. Among these diverse types are historical narrative, prophecy, poetry, wisdom literature, apocalyptic literature, parable, the proverb, Gospel records, letters and typology. To each type of material there are proper rules for interpreting it.

When Jesus tells the parable of the unjust judge, He does not intend to represent God in this character; indeed, just the opposite. As is true of some parables (but not all of them) there is but one point made. In this instance, it is God's response to fervent constancy in prayer. Many persons who fail to recognize the duplicatory nature of much Hebrew parallelism (the basic form that underlies Hebrew poetry, many proverbs, and even some rhetorically emotional biblical preaching) misinterpret passages as a result.

Take for instance Psalm 108:3, 4, 5:

I will praise Thee, O Lord, Among the peoples,
I will chant praises to Thee among the nations.
For Thy lovingkindness is higher than the heavens,
and Thy faithfulness soars to the skies.

Be Thou exalted, O God, beyond the heavens,
and may Thy glory tower over all the earth!

Clearly, in each verse, the second line repeats the first in slightly different words. It is easy enough to recognize this phenomenon in verses like that. But now consider the following:

> ...a generation which did not prepare its heart;
> and its spirit was not faithful to God
> (Ps. 78:8[b], Berkeley).

Many fail to recognize that in this verse, as in so many others, *spirit* is paralleled with *heart*.[1] Instead of saying that the point of the passage is reinforced by the repetition, they distinguish between things that, instead, ought to be identified.

Sometimes the existence of synonymous parallelism provides valuable, additional information or even the clue to an otherwise difficult-to-interpret line or two. In Proverbs 2:17, the wife who forsakes the husband of her youth is the same as the one who forgets God's covenant. From this parallelism, in which one line greatly amplifies the next, we judge that marriage is a covenant. That parallelism and Exodus 16:8[b] (Berkeley), where marriage is further explained as entering into a covenant, strongly set forth this covenantal nature of marriage. Plainly, valuable facts may be deduced from the juxtaposition of parallel concepts that amplify or complement one another.

Consider this:

> He who covers an offense seeks love
> (Prov. 17:9[a], Berkeley)

What does that mean? Does he seek to obtain someone's love by overlooking his sins? Is that the way to develop friendships? The second half of the verse provides the clue that explains the first:

---

1. Cf. also Ps. 64:6[b]: "...for the inner man and the heart are fathomless" (Berkeley); identification, not distinction, is required. See Ps. 13:2, where heart and soul are in parallel to each other.

But he who brings up the matter again, alienates a close friend.

The whole verse is speaking of someone who will not allow a matter to die. Rather than teaching that one should refuse to raise a matter at all (a notion that contradicts other passages of Scripture), the second line shows that the verse refers to a situation in which the matter was properly disposed of (by rebuke and forgiveness presumably) and ought to be buried forever. The one half of the verse clarifies the other.

Rhetorical studies of various sorts are informative and essential for correct interpretation. It is necessary to know something about these and to be prepared to do such study when you come to a passage in which the form of the material in some way or another has influence over the interpretation.

THEOLOGICAL INTERPRETATION

Biblical theology teaches us to make sure that every passage is viewed in the light of Christ's redemptive work. To ask, "How does the cross apply to this passage?" is the way to avoid moralizing and self-help approaches.

Moreover, the use of a systematic approach to the Bible keeps one from wrongly using any given passages as though it were the only word on the subject. In *More than Redemption* I wrote:

> In its simplest form, theology is nothing more or less than the systematic understanding of what the Scriptures teach about various subjects. Biblical passages concerning any subject—let us say, the teaching of the Bible about God—are located, exegeted in context, placed into the stream of the history of redemption and their teachings classified according to the several aspects of that subject (God's omnipotence, omniscience, omnipresence, for instance). Within

each classification, these teachings are compared to one another (one passage supplementing and qualifying another) in order to discover the total scriptural teaching on this aspect of the doctrine. Each aspect, likewise, is compared to other aspects in order to understand the total scriptural teaching about that question (and various subjects also are studied in relation to each other for further amplifications and modifications according to the light that one subject throws upon another). Thus, simply stated, theology is the attempt to bring to bear upon any given doctrine (or teaching) all that the Bible has to say about it. Biblical theology also notes the development of special revelation particularly in relationship to the redemptive work of Christ. And the individual theologies of the various writers of biblical books must be studied and related to one another too.[1] All of these elements are of concern to us in this book.

Let me partially demonstrate how theology can influence practical living by one brief example. In John 14:13,14, Jesus says, "I will do whatever you ask in my name....If you ask Me anything, I will do it." By itself, that statement seems to constitute a *carte blanche* in prayer. (And too often those who have little concern for theology have taken it that way; they have preached and counseled, saying, "Whatever you want you can get by praying for it.") As a result of a failure to use theology in the exegesis of the passage (asking, for instance, "What does the important qualification, 'in My name,' mean—

---

1. Not that their basic theological beliefs differ, but frequently their use of terminology does. These differences must be harmonized.

how is the phrase used elsewhere?"[1] and, "What other qualifications do other Scriptures place upon prayer?"), many Christians have been misled and have been deeply disappointed when they tried to use prayer as an open sesame to unlock their problems and satisfy their desires. They discover—the hard way—that prayer doesn't work that way. Adequate theological study would take into account such passages as John 16:23, 24, 26, 27; Philippians 4:6, 7; James 4:2, 3; 5:15-18 when referring to John 14:13, 14. The qualifications in these references—even if not mentioned to the counselee—must be known (and kept in mind) by the counselor whenever he speaks about John 14:13,14, so that he will not convey a wrong impression (i.e., an atheological, simplistic one) to the counselee.[2]

---

1. For example, in John 15:21
2. Pp. 11, 12.

9

PRINCIPLES OF BIBLICAL INTERPRETATION

Because it is important to become familiar with principles for interpreting the Bible. I have devoted this chapter to a summary of some of the major concepts of which you should be aware.

What is a correct interpretation? A correct interpretation is one that accurately mirrors the thought that God had in mind and inscripturated by inspiration. An interpretation must be complete in order to be correct. If it is but partial, and not the whole truth, it may be misleading. A complete interpretation satisfies all legitimate questions that can be raised.[1] A correct interpretation must be *consistent* with the rest of Scripture. All truth is systematic and consistent. In short, a correct interpretation gets out of a passage exactly what God put into it.

I. General Principles Of Biblical Interpretation[2]
   A. Assumptions:
      1. The Scriptures are perspicuous; they are not a puzzle designed to deceive and confuse, but rather a revelation (lit., "unveiling") of God's truth about Himself, man, and creation in their relationships to one another, designed to enlighten, convince and move to action.
      2. The Scriptures are inspired throughout—in language as well as thought—and are, therefore, without error.

---

1. I.e. all questions that do not violate the proscription in Deut. 29:29.
2. The outline in this chapter may be used as the basis for a course of study in a Bible class, a college course or a Sunday school course.

3. The Scriptures are sufficient, teaching all that one needs to love God and his neighbor.

B. There is only one correct interpretation of any passage.

   1. Cf. *The Westminster Confession of Faith* (I:9): "The true and full sense of any scripture...is not manifold, but one."

   2. Contrast the errors of Swedenborgians (fourfold sense of Scripture) and allegorizing by Christian Scientists, etc.

C. The laws of grammar must be observed.

   1. God gave us His revelation in written language. He expects us to know something of the parts of speech and their use.

   2. Cf. Galatians 3:16, where Paul hangs an entire argument upon a singular noun ("seed...not seeds").

   3. We should understand the meanings of punctuation with respect to the Bible (KJV punctuation was not grammatical; it was punctuation for reading out loud; it does not follow grammatical rules.)

D. Proper use of reason and logic must be used in interpreting the Scriptures.

   1. *The Westminster Confession of Faith* (I:6) states that we are to obey the Scriptures as our rule of faith and life according to what is "either expressly set down" or by "good and necessary consequence may be deduced from Scripture."

   2. This important principle recognizes that God is a God of order and system and that His truth is necessarily systematic and self-consistent.

   3. The Scriptures are never unreasonable or illogical, though at times they may speak about that which is *beyond* human reason and logic (e.g., the Trinity is not illogical or unreasonable, but is beyond our full comprehension).

4. Note Acts 2:25-31 as an example of reasoning used by Peter in interpreting and applying Old Testament Scripture.

E. Scripture itself should be the primary guide for interpreting Scripture.

1. Whenever possible, other Scriptures should be consulted in interpretation.

2. Scripture is the only "infallible" interpreter of Scripture (Cf. *Westminster Confession of Faith* (I:9).

3. Warning: be sure, however, that so-called or seemingly parallel passages are *really* parallel. The mere use of the same word, example or phrase in two or more contexts does not prove these to be parallel in *usage*. Be careful to distinguish *verbal* parallels from *real* ones (thought and subject identity). Leaven in Matthew 13:33ff., does not have an evil connotation because it is also used of Pharisaical doctrine. The point of similarity is not evil, but the power of a little of something to permeate the whole ("a little leaven leavens the whole lump").

4. Cf. The problem of "tongues" in I Corinthians 14 is clarified by Acts 2, which throws much light on this passage. There the *nature* of the gift is clearly indicated as the ability to speak in foreign languages.

F. Discover true divisions, transitions, etc.

1. Learn to question man-made divisions (verses, chapters, punctuation). None of these are inspired (they were added hundreds of years later for convenience).

2. Modern Bibles, which are paragraphed, are more accurate and helpful, but still the paragraphing is not inspired.

3. I Corinthians 12-14 is all one unit; because of the presence of chapter headings, the love poem in chapter 13 has been unnaturally divorced from the context.

    4. Isaiah 52:13-15 is the beginning of the material found in chapter 53.

    5. Colossians 3:16: The comma should follow "another."

G. Italics should be read intelligently.

    1. They are not used in the King James Version as they are in modern printing (for emphasis). Rather, they indicate words not in the original, supplied by the translators to help give *what they thought* (but were by no means sure) was the sense of the passage.

    2. Cf. John 8:6: Here these italics are pure opinion. They *may* be correct or not. Perhaps it was WHAT Christ wrote that was important. Cf. John 18:6 with Exodus 3:14 to see how the italicized words destroy the fact that Christ was pronouncing the name of Jehovah in reference to Himself.

H. The context always must be consulted. "Context" means "a weaving together." It refers to the web of the passage. Almost all verses have a context (most Proverbs are exceptions).

    1. John Wycliffe (1324-1384) long ago wrote: "It shall greatly help ye to understand Scripture, if thou mark not only what is spoken or written, but of whom, and to whom, with what words, at what time, where, to what interest, with what circumstances, considering what goeth before and what followeth."

    2. "Context" may mean *immediate* context (i.e., the few verses before or after, which form the paragraph in which the verse occurs), or the *more distant* context (i.e., the whole topic under discussion, which may take up several paragraphs, an *entire* book, or even lead beyond to other books.) Cf. the prayer in Luke 23:34. Was the prayer heard? Yes. Read Acts 2:13-15 for the confirmation of this fact.

3. This principle is so important that several examples must be studied:

    a. Romans 8:28 is a marvelous promise, but the immediate context must be consulted to discover the persons who qualify for its provisions.

    b. Hebrews 6:4-6 seems to say that persons once saved can be lost. But verses 7-9 (esp. v. 9) indicate that such people never were saved.

    c. The interpretation of various portions of the Book of Revelation depends upon the time and purposes for which it was written.

    d. Philippians 4:4-7 has much more meaning when compared with 1:13.

    e. Isaiah 14:12-15 is a good example. Going back to verse 4 (the beginning of the immediate context) and continuing through verse 28 (the end of the immediate context), a careful student cannot fail to see that this passage, which is frequently applied to Satan, in reality is a very poetic prophecy of the rise and fall of the king of Babylon.

I. The literal must be distinguished from the figurative.

    1. Take this sentence: "The moon is a silver fish swimming through a sea of clouds." Is it literal or figurative? How do we determine if it is a "metaphor" (i.e., a figure of speech in which one thing is likened to a another)?

    2. Principles for determining what is literal and what is figurative:

        a. When the literal is absurd, try the figurative: e.g., Psalm 91:4, "He shall cover thee with feathers, and under his wings shalt thou trust." God is not a cosmic bird. The figure combines both cognitive and evocative elements. Here they are care, warmth, love, protection, etc. By a figure often *more* can be conveyed. A figure is both denotative and connotative. But often the solution is not so simple.

b. If it is not quite so easy, try the literal interpretation, and test it against the teaching of other clear passages. If it does not harmonize, try the figurative.

c. Examine internal indication:

(1) Ask what type of literature the passage is. Poetic (much figurative language here)? Apocalyptic (which is largely symbolic in literary form)? Narrative? Historical? Prophetical (much of this is in poetic form)?

(2) Are there any keys in the book itself? E.g., Revelation 1 already indicates that it contains symbols that must stand for other things (the stars and the lampstands are interpreted as symbolic: cf. 1:20).

(3) But figures teach factual, literal and historical truth. In the vision of the metallic image in Daniel, figures stood for five literal, historical kingdoms: Babylon, Medo-Persia, Greece, Rome and the kingdom of heaven.

J. Do not overlook the author's own interpretations:

1. Cf. Revelation 17:7-18. The angel is sent to "tell...the mystery" (or "explain" the mystery). That this is a phrase indicating the interpretation of a symbolic figure is clear from its prior use in 1:20.

2. Cf. Daniel 8:20-26.

K. Remember the principle of progressive revelation.

1. Scripture was revealed over a long period of time in successive epochs (cf. Heb. 1:1)

2. The movement was not from error to truth, but from truth to greater truth.

3. The Old Testament was a story without an ending. It looked *forward* to the New Testament for its climax and meaning. It was the foundation upon which the New Testament is built. Christ is the subject of both the Old Testament and the New Testament.

4. Therefore, earlier revelations must be read in the light of later ones (on the same subject) for *our* application *today*, but not for interpretation of the passage in its context. Rather, to find the principles intended for the original readers of the revelation itself, one must put himself back into the shoes of those who received it.

5. In II Kings 10:18-27 there is recorded Jehu's destruction of the priests of Baal. That at this period God worked through a divinely governed monarchy makes some of the factors in the passage directly inapplicable to our time. Today Christ's kingdom is "not of this world"; thus his servants no longer promote it by warfare (John 18:36). But the underlying principles remain, regardless of the shifting forms in which they appear. The principles are clear, and are applicable to our time, but only after adjustment, by relating them to this change in the divine economy. It would be wrong either (1) to change into consideration, or (2) to ignore the principles in such passages as totally inapplicable to us (cf. I Cor. 10:11). Both extremes are wrong.

L. Avoid any *brand-new* interpretations.

1. Although it is *possible* that you will be the first to fully understand the passage involved, it is unlikely that everyone else has been wrong for so long.

2. The Spirit is at work in others besides you.

3. No cult would have developed had the founders followed this rule.

M. A negative approach is often helpful.
   1. Often it is easier to proceed by the process of elimination.
   2. Examination and rejection of all the other possibilities often leads one directly to the truth.
   3. Warning: Be sure rejections are made on a solid basis, not because of subjective factors.
N. Word study can be helpful.
   1. Sometimes the Greek has several words for the sole English term used to render them. Cf. "world" in the King James Version: I John 2:15, Luke 4:5, and I Corinthians 10:11 in the Greek are: *Kosmos* (world, arrangement, universe, system of things), *oikoumene* (Mediterranean civilization, the civilized world), and *aion* (age, era), successively.
   2. Word usages should be determined from their usage in the Scriptures, wherever adequate indications of the usage are present to help.
   3. "Root" meanings can be deceptive. The meaning of the word *at the time it was written* is the important factor.
   4. Strong's concordance can be helpful.
   5. Word study can be important in understanding different shades of meaning: e.g. in the New Testament there are 10 distinct words for sin, each with its distinct denotations and connotations (Cf. *More than Redemption* for a word study of each).
O. Pursue a well-rounded emphasis in the study of the whole counsel of God.
   1. Some go overboard for one kind of study (e.g., prophecy). They ride hobbies and neglect many important areas of truth. Cf. Acts 20:27.
   2. The Old Testament is often neglected, especially the Proverbs and the Psalms: "The Psalms tell us how to

live toward God, the Proverbs teach us how to live toward man" (Lindleigh Roberts).

P. Imagination.

1. There is both wealth and danger here. The use of imagination is essential and needs cultivation and limitation.

2. The ability to "picture" situations, descriptions, makes Scripture "live." This is, in a sense, reading between the lines, but it is also *truly* reading the lines too.

3. The danger is in reading *into* the text what is *not* there.

4. Aids to imagination may be found in the study of history, archaeology, Bible geography, Bible customs and manners, etc.

5. Read John 2:13-17. Picture the circumstances. Imagine what money changers looked like, smell the stench from the animals, listen to the noise and haggling, see the doves flying around and the money spilling all over the place, don't miss the confusion, anger, fear, etc. Unless you have some imagination (the ability to see), you don't truly interpret.

Q. Learn abstract principles.

1. It is necessary to learn how to abstract the general principle(s) contained in the specific passage so that these may be applied to new specific problems today.

2. Study Romans 14 and abstract the general principles involved in that context where the specific problem had to do with food offered to idols. What are they? Name some current problems to which these principles may be applied.

R. Don't sacrifice thoroughness and care for speed.

1. Take adequate time while applying maximum effort and precision when interpreting.

2. It is better to come to *no* conclusion than to the *wrong* one.

3. Sometimes it is wise to lay a study aside until a later point.
   a. Then it can be approached from a fresher viewpoint;
   b. Perhaps it can be interpreted only after other more basic (or collateral) studies have been made.

4. Don't hesitate to admit it when you cannot come to an answer.

S. When interpreting the words or actions of evil persons, or persons speaking or acting sinfully, these words should not be applied as precepts or examples to follow:

1. Cf. Job 1:9, 10 (Satan's words); also many of the words of his "friends."

2. In Ecclesiastes 3:18-22 the writer speaks as an unsaved man would.

3. These are inspired words; i.e., without error they faithfully tell us what Satan or evil men said but do not purport to provide advice to be followed.

II. Special Principles Of Bible Interpretation
A. Parables

1. The word means "a throwing alongside of" and indicates that a truth is presented in terms of a story that illustrates and embodies the truth.

2. There is only *one* truth taught by some parables. They are unlike the allegory, in which many factors are parallel and each part of the story signifies something.

3. Cf. Matthew 13:31-32; 33. What is the point?

4. Christ used parables to reveal and conceal: Matthew 13:34-35 (reveals truths to those with ears to hear);

Matthew 13:13-16 (conceals them from those who wouldn't hear properly).

B. Prophecy

1. Prophecy is intended to be a light in a dark place (II Pet. 1:19).

2. There is no reason for believing that prophecies have a double fulfillment.

3. Some prophecy is conditional (cf. the rule in Jer. 18:7-10)

4. Some is literal; some is figurative: cf. Genesis 3:15 and Malachi 4:5—both the first and last prophecies of the Old Testament are figurative.

5. Most prophecy cannot be *fully* understood until after it has been fulfilled: the order is prophecy, fact, interpretation.

C. Typology

1. What is a "type"? The word meant a print, a mark or impress made by a hard substance upon a softer one; then, it came to mean a model, pattern or exemplar; finally, it means a representative character or object. In Romans 5:14 "figure" is literally "type"; also, in I Corinthians 10:11 "examples" is "type."

2. The important point to remember is that <u>there must be more than a resemblance for something to be a genuine type:</u> The type is *designed* as such by God. God must have designed it to represent or prefigure something else in at least one respect.

   a. New Testament usage alone can be a certain guide for determining such design.

   b. There are other types than those clearly labeled by the New Testament. We may determine what these are by noting how the New Testament writers identified types.

   c. Cf. Hebrews 10:1; 8:5; Colossians 2:6.

    d. Melchizedek was a symbol: The type is always something (someone) real and historical, whereas a symbol may not be.

3. The "antitype" (I Pet. 3:21) is that of which something else is a type; it is the reality itself.

4. Doctrines should not be determined but only illustrated by types.

5. Types may be found in persons (Melchizedek), events (crossing the Red Sea), structures (the ark, tabernacle), furniture (alter, laver), ritual (offerings, festivals), clothing (robes, priestly garments) and rules (clean, unclean).

D. Allegory

1. Definition: saying another thing from that which is meant. It is an extended metaphor, whereas the parable is an extended simile.

2. There is one clear instance in the New Testament: Galatians 4:21. The word is used only there.

3. Paul uses the word to appeal to Jews (who used allegory frequently) to show them that even by their own methods his point was true. Paul meets the Judaizers and Pharisees on their own grounds.

E. Symbolism

1. A symbol is an object or picture that stands for something. This object need not be real or historical as a type is. Symbols are in the spiritual realm what cartoons are in the political: cf. the donkey and elephant, which stand for the Democratic and Republican Parties, and Uncle Sam for the U.S.A.

2. E.g., Revelation

    a. The Lamb = Christ (5:6ff).

    b. The dragon = Satan (12:3; 12:9)

    c. The harlot = Rome (17:18).

    d. The radiant woman = the church (12:13-14).

e.   The city of Babylon = Rome (17:5).

f.   The New Jerusalem = heaven (21:2)

F. Poetry

   1. Its characteristics: exaggerations, the extreme, person-ification, vividness, picturesqueness.

   2. Its form:

     a.   The poetic form in Hebrew is repetitive "parallel-ism."

     b.   Cf. Psalms and Proverbs, especially Psalm 2:1, 3, 5, 9, 10; Psalm 1:5.

     c.   Read Numbers 23:8, 9. Read only every other clause and you will find that it makes perfect sense. It will be prose that you are reading. Now put in the omitted clauses and you will be reading poetry.

     d.   The second clause in a poetic parallel usually says the same thing as the first in other (similar) words, or emphasizes the point by stating the antithesis to it, or the implications of it.

     e.   The basic value of knowing this:

       (1) No rigid distinctions should be made between variant terms in separate clauses.

       (2) If one clause is difficult to understand, then, in synonymous parallelism, the other often explains it.

G. Handling Apparent Contradictions

   1. Basic assumptions

     a.   No man knowingly is inconsistent.

     b.   All possible harmonies should be attempted instead of declaring even uninspired works incon-sistent.

     c.   In the case of *Scripture*, the writers were pre-served from error; there are no true contradic-tions.

2. In many cases *more information* will clear up a seeming contradiction.
3. Many of the supposed contradictions have been solved for centuries. Cf. Haley's *Alleged Discrepancies* (Baker Book House).

H. Numerology

1. Paninism sees all Scripture as based on numbers. Ivan Panin tries to determine the best manuscript readings etc., on this basis. This is an extreme to avoid.
2. Certain numbers *do* take on biblical significance:

   a. Seven shows completeness (as in the *full cycle* of the week). It shows God's hand in something (as creation). Also multiples of 7=70 disciples, weeks.

   b. Twelve and multiples (24, 144,000): the numbers of the church—12 tribes; 12 apostles; cf. Revelation 21:12-14.

   c. Three=Trinity. Also, Christ was three days in the earth. A true unity.

   d. Forty days and nights: the flood: Moses on Sinai; years of wilderness wandering; Christ's fast. Seems to be a testing, preparatory, or transition period.

   e. There are others, but these seem most important. Note: the letters of the Greek and Hebrew alphabets were used for numbers; each had a numerical value.

CONCLUSION

The foregoing principles are elementary, but should afford a working basis for personal Bible study. If followed carefully, they will open new insights for the faithful student.

10

INTERPRETING FOR INTENT

Discovering the intent of the Holy Spirit in a passage ought to be the basic goal of all scriptural interpretation.

The *telos* (or purpose) of the passage should be central to everything that is done in Bible study; that means that it is the vital factor even in the selection of the passage *as appropriate* to the problem at hand.

The *telic* side of study has been either ignored, underplayed, or unknown by many. Many have persisted in using the Scriptures for their own purposes rather than for the purposes for which they were given. Often because blissfully unaware of the Holy Spirit's intention in placing a passage where it occurs, they have generated the most incredible interpretations and dogmas and have given some of the most horrendous advice, all in the name of God.

Scriptural authority arises from knowing that the interpretation you adopt truly comes from God. That cannot be known unless you are sure that a directive, warning, or promise comes from the Scriptures. The authority will be lacking unless (a) you know the *telos* of the passage and (b) use it for the same purpose as that for which the Holy Spirit gave it. Because the matter under discussion is of such vital importance, I shall linger for a while over each of those necessary elements in establishing scriptural authority for living. With Paul, you must be able to say in good conscience, "For I do not, like so many, peddle an adulterated message of God" (II Cor. 2:17).

(a) You must know the *telos* of every passage that you study. It is not enough to understand the grammatical-historical, biblical-theological or systematic, literary and rhetorical aspects of a passage. These are important, and I should be the last one to say anything to undermine such work, for each of these elements may play a vital part in biblical interpretation. Indeed, without their assistance often it is impossible either to discover the *telos* or to be sure even when one has done so. Yet it is possible to have all these matters in mind and still *misuse* a portion of Scripture in preaching or counseling. Thus, the story of the Seeking Father and the Pouting Elder Brother instead, when misinterpreted, becomes the Parable of the Prodigal Son. The two commandments to love God and neighbor are psychologized by those who want to add to them a third commandment, "love yourself," which they then make basic to the other two, in spite of the fact that this is a thought repugnant to the entire Bible, and the clear statement of Christ that He is speaking of *two* commandments only: "On these *two* commandments hang all the law and the prophets."

(b) The counselor must know the *purpose* of the passage; that is, he must know what God intended to do to the reader (warn, encourage, motivate, etc.) with those words. Then, he must make God's purpose his own in the application of the passage to human needs. But to do this he must develop an interpretive conscience by which he determines never to use a passage for any purpose other than that purpose, or those purposes for which God gave it (often, of course, there are sub*tele* involved in a larger telic unit). This determination will make him faithful not only as an interpreter, but also in his *use* of the Scriptures.

(c) The Scriptures must be "opened" (i.e., "explained," cf. Luke 24:32) if you would have your heart burn within you like the hearts of the disciples who walked the Emmaus road with Christ. When *He* is disclosed as the subject of "all" of the Scriptures, moralizing will disappear, irrelevant material will evaporate and the *telos* of the passage will find its proper place in Christ.

But how does one discover the *telos* of any passage? (1) By studying with the *telic* goal in mind (one rarely finds what he does not seek), and in that search (2) by looking for *telic* cues. Often these cues are overt; but some are more evident than others. Some *telic* statements have to do with the *whole* of Scriptures, as for example when Paul wrote that the Scriptures have two purposes: "to make one wise unto salvation" and to "teach, convict, correct, and train in righteousness" (II Tim. 3:15-16). Thus any given passage primarily will have either an evangelistic or edificational goal. In Luke 24:27, Christ referred to Himself as the subject of "all of the Scriptures," which is perhaps the most basic and comprehensive *telos* of all. Christ Himself is the Savior and Head of His church who has made salvation and Christian growth a reality. The Christian, therefore, must see Christ in every passage that he uses. This means that he may never use the Scriptures moralistically or humanistically.

John's Gospel and first epistle provide the most obvious sorts of *telic* notes: the first was "written...that you may *believe*," and the second "written to you who believe...that you may *know*." Is there any wonder then that verses like John 1:12; 3:16; 3:36; 5:24; 14:1-6 and many others have been used so frequently by the Spirit of God to bring men to belief? After all, the Gospel of John, we are clearly told, was written for this purpose. Likewise one should turn to the first epistle for assurance of salvation.

Portions of Biblical books are devoted to different purposes. When the writer of Hebrews says, "Therefore leaving the elementary teaching about Christ, let us press on..." (6:1), he is giving the reader a *telic* cue to a shift in emphasis (all, of course, within the scope of the broader *telos or tele* for which the book of Hebrews was written). Ephesians 1-3 cannot be separated from Ephesians 4-6, since the two sections are hinged together by that crucial "therefore" in Ephesians 4:1 which shows that the doctrine taught in the first half has vital implications for the practical Christian living enjoined in the second half. Yet, it is important to know that the latter portion of Ephesians shows *how* Christians, as members of Christ's redeemed body (the theme of the former), can learn to function together in love and unity.

Phrases like "Brethren, I would not have you ignorant concerning..." (I Thess. 4:13); "Wherefore, comfort one another with these words" (I Thess. 4:18); "I have written...to encourage you and to testify that this is the true grace of God" (I Pet. 5:12); "I wish, therefore, always to remind you of these matters...(II Pet. 1:12, 13);" I am writing you to arouse your pure minds by way of remembrance" (II Pet. 3:1); "I found it necessary to write you appealing that you vigorously defend the faith once for all delivered to the saints" (Jude 3); "prescribe and teach these things" (I Tim. 4:11); "remind them of these things and solemnly charge them in the presence of God..." (II Tim. 2:14) are just a few of the many *telic* cues by which the counselor can be guided infallibly in determining the Holy Spirit's intentions in any given passage of the Scriptures.

Even when *telic* cues do not appear overtly, the *telic* quest still must be carried on. And this quest may be pursued successfully, for although the *tele* may not always be as apparent as in the New Testament examples mentioned above, they may be found by looking for *telic* thrusts and emphases. Thus, for example, there are few overt *telic* cues in Philippians, but the student who seeks to discover the main *tele* behind the writing of that book will have little trouble uncovering such purposes as (a) Paul's desire to thank the Philippians for their gift, (b) his concern to explain the working of God's providence in his imprisonment, (c) his interest in healing the division in the Philippian church, and (d) his wish to calm their fears about Epaphroditus.

Now everything that I said there of the telic study of the Scriptures for counseling holds equally well for the Bible interpretation that you will do in your daily study. You will not let a passage go until you have determined the purpose or the intent of the Holy Spirit in giving it.

Let us sum up some of the most important facts about purpose:

1. A unit of Scripture is a *telic* (or purpose) unit.
2. The books of the Bible, the various sections and subsections, all have *tele* (purposes) or sub-*tele*.
3. The *telos* or sub-*telos* of a passage is the intent of the Spirit in giving the passage.
4. This intent or purpose must be discovered by the grammatical, historical, rhetorical, cultural and theological studies that ought to be made, not as an end in themselves, but as a means used to discover the *telos* of the passage.
5. The passage must be used in meeting life's problems only for the purpose, or purposes, for which it was given.

Keeping these five principles in mind will go a long way toward directing you in the right path in Bible interpretation. Apart from them, one is prone to wander astray before long.

PART FOUR

BIBLICAL ~~INTERPRETATION~~
Implementation

11

IMPLEMENTATION IN GENERAL

We have seen that to use the Bible adequately, one needs Bible information. He must be able to find his way around in the Bible and must have a systematic grasp on various categories of biblical principles. He must be able to locate a wide variety of passages that apply to all of life. He also must acquire and use correct principles and practices of Bible interpretation. The ability to interpret well comes through the regular use of proper practices in proper ways. Regular means use on a daily basis. Regular practice will yield much more biblical information and will help one develop habitual attitudes and procedures of biblical interpretation while, at the same time, keeping him in touch daily with what God is saying to him in His Word. It will also remind him to use his Bible every day—including Thursday. But we are not yet through; there remains another factor: Bible implementation.

It is essential to know how to locate all the truth from the Bible that is needed to deal with an issue or problem. Similarly, it is important to be able to interpret each passage properly, discovering its *telos*. But all of this—even when it has been done well—can fall flat and effect little or nothing unless what has been learned is coupled with proper implementation. Implementation is what gets the job done.

But, more precisely, what is implementation? It is *adaptation* of biblical truth for biblical purposes, in practical ways, according to a biblical derived *plan and schedule,* together with biblical, or biblically legitimate methods for meeting the schedule, to a specific person in his individual circumstances.

In the preceding paragraph, I italicized several words. These matters must be taken up separately; each is important in itself. I have written something about implementation elsewhere (see especially *Ready to Restore* and *Creativity in Christian Counseling),* and I shall not repeat what I have said there from a different perspective. Instead, I want to supplement that material and to recast the entire discussion in a different mold.

Implementation is a matter of works. Both Paul and James alike taught that true faith always leads to works that are pleasing to God. But one of the problems among Christians today is that they don't know *how* to move from faith to works. You often see faith struggling to get loose, but being frustrated by an inability to express itself in concrete deeds. That is largely because of the modern conservative church's lopsided emphasis on faith to the exclusion of works. As a result, we are consequently concerned with the *what* to the exclusion of *how.* Consequently, there are many Christians who want to please God, who want to but do not know where to begin. Of course, that is no excuse for their not beginning anywhere. They should not give up but ask and study until they discover the how. On the other hand the church has been failing to point the way to the implementation of biblical obligations.

The church has featured facts to the exclusion of ways and means. While either one of these factors can be overemphasized, it is time, it seems, to talk a lot more about ways and means (but not in a reactionary way that would swing the pendulum to the opposite extreme). God does not want us to become fact-filled Christians who never use those facts, through neglect or lack of know-how. Truth is designed to "bring about godliness," as Paul told Titus. And James said, "Who is wise and intelligent among you? Let him show this by his behavior, by his works done in wise meekness" (James 3:13). Wisdom is not knowledge; it is knowledge meekly used in life.

In this forth part of the book, therefore, I shall outline a procedure for implementing the biblical answers that you receive after you have located and interpreted them.

Of course, it is not enough just to get a job done; God cares about how it is done and about what is happening in the life of the one who is doing it. He is interested not only in results, but in methods and in men. That is why, for instance, He tells us that we will be "made happy in the doing" (James 1:25c).

With God, the end does not justify the means. All of the ways and means that you use to accomplish God's will must also be according to God's will. The motives and the attitudes in which you do what God requires are significant. Ways and means, therefore, must be biblically directed or biblically derived. Intent must be biblically defensible at all points.

What do I mean by the distinction between *biblically directed* and *biblically derived* methods? A biblically directed method is a method specifically prescribed as such in the Bible; a biblically derived method is a method devised by the Christian himself in accordance with and within the framework of biblical principles in order to fulfill a biblical command to which there is attached no biblically directed method.

When God forbade worship by means of idols and instead required temple worship through sacrifices and offerings in carefully prescribed ways, not only was He requiring Old Testament saints to worship Him, but He was also telling them how to do so. No Israelite could decide, on his own, to invent some novel method of worship. The method itself had been prescribed by God. Failure to follow His will in the use of divinely directed ways and means was judged as severely as a failure to set forth and to achieve proper ends and goals. Methods that were unbiblical could be characterized, as, for instance, "strange fire" (Lev. 10:1). The judgment for such unauthorized action was swift and deadly (cf. v. 2; see also II Sam. 6:6, 7; Num. 4:15). God thereby taught His people that He would not tolerate methods growing out of human innovation and used in the place of divinely revealed and directed ones.

"But that was in the Old Testament," you may protest. Yes, it was, and while it is true that God has given us who live in New Testament times no such elaborate details about methods of worship or about everyday living, nevertheless, it is possible for us also to innovate in ways that are displeasing to Him.

One such form of innovation against which we are warned is "will worship," or, as the original word might be translated, "self-imposed worship" (Col. 2:23). In self-imposed worship, ideas from the world (v. 20) are laid down as requirements even though God did not require them. These ascetic requirements in Colossi (vv. 21-23 detail them for you) were devised by man, and not by God. They remind one of the prohibition that Eve added to the divine command: "Neither shall you touch it" (Gen. 3:3). This statement was the first evidence of Eve's defection from the pure simplicity of God's revealed Word. God opposes any human commandments that are set forth *on the same level as* His commandments. So, our first principle is this:

> When God has prescribed what we must do, we may not add to His requirements.

This is an important point to remember in any discussion of implementation because there is always the danger of adopting humanly derived ways or means—even if otherwise in keeping with biblical principles—in place of divinely ordained ones. It is also dangerous to *require* any human regulation of another. Only God-given commandments may be required of a believer. Moreover, according to Colossians 2:23, we may not even make such requirements *for ourselves*. It is very important never to subject yourself to any commandment of men as if it were on the same level with a divine commandment.

Does that mean that we may never commit ourselves to a course of action that we (or some other Christians) devise in order to fulfill a command of God? If so, wouldn't that eliminate implementation altogether? Yes, it would.

But commitment to proper implementation of biblical commands, when no implementation is spelled out in the Bible, is quite a different thing from requiring and imposing rules and regulations. The key factor is that no biblically derived implementation may be granted divine status. It is a human method that you are devising; not a divinely given one. Humanly derived ways and means are subject to us; when they are divinely given, we are subject to them. The former may be altered, abandoned in favor of others, supplemented; the latter may not. It is imposing human rules as though they carried divine authority that is forbidden in Colossians 2:23.

Yet the warning is pertinent. Human ideas, even when properly conceived and instituted, in time can take on an authority that does not belong to them. That was the problem with the Pharisees, who placed the tradition of men on the same level with the Scriptures and thus made the Bible of no effect. That tradition may have begun as implementation of biblical precepts. Soon it became as authoritative to them as Scriptures, and eventually replaced God's Word. Ideas, good in themselves, after a while may become evil because their status is elevated beyond that of mere implementation of a divine commandment to a status equal to the commandment itself.

In the process, the implementation may become frozen and soon looked on as the only proper way to fulfill the command. An example of this is the Wednesday night prayer meeting. Corporate prayer is commanded, and Wednesday night prayer is a good thing, but there is no biblical injunction to meet for prayer on Wednesday night. Persons who berate others for nonattendance must be careful, therefore, that they themselves do not fall into the condemnation of Colossians 2:23.

In our discussion we have ranged from consideration of the substitution of evil human ways and means for divinely revealed procedures to the distortion and misuse of proper biblically derived implementation that has been frozen and elevated to the status of a divine command. Both must be avoided. The danger can be detected by asking, "If I don't do it this way (an implementation of a command), will others, or will I, consider it a sin?" The failure to follow humanly devised implementation can, in itself, never be considered a sin, though there are times when under special conditions it may be (e.g., when one has made a promise to another to do something in a particular way, and "doesn't feel like it"). One important way to keep from elevating a human method to the status of a divine command is to be sure to think of more than one way to implement the command that God did give. Multiplicity of methods, all biblically derived, of course, is one of the surest safeguards against this danger.

This discussion now leads us to ask a further question: "You have assumed that it is proper for us to devise ways and means for implementing those divine commands that have no biblical directions for fulfilling them included. But are you sure that even that sort of implementation is legitimate?" The answer is yes. Listen to the following words found in Titus 2:2-5:

> Older women, similarly, must be taught to conduct themselves with an outward bearing that is appropriate to holy persons, not being slanders, nor slaves of much wine. They must be teachers of what is good so that they may train the young women to show affection to their husbands and to their children, to be self-restrained, pure, housekeepers, kind, submitting themselves to their husbands, that God's Word may not be blasphemed.

Notice two things:

1. Titus was commanded to teach older women to teach younger women. But he is not told how to do so. Is he to hold older women's Bible classes? Is he to teach them one by one?

The command itself carries no indication of the method for fulfilling it. When younger men are to be taught, Titus is told that at least one way in which he is to do this teaching is by the example of his own life (2:6-8). But he is given no such direction for the women.

2. Titus was to teach the older women to be teachers of good things (v. 3) and to train[1] the younger women to do such things as show affection for their husbands, be housekeepers and submit. It is clear that Titus was not to do this by example. All he could do was to "speak" about it to them (2:1). But should he do this informally, formally? With the younger women present, or not? The ways and means for accomplishing these several tasks simply are not spelled out. Titus, and the older women after him, were left to their own ingenuity to decide how best to implement these directions.

There are many such commands in the Bible. In such cases, He expects us to use the brains that He gave us. That is why this section is important.

But I have mentioned not only that the Biblically derived methods for fulfilling God's teaching at all points (older women, for instance, could not teach younger ones by bringing in pagan Cretan women to lecture them about their concepts of child rearing), but also that God is concerned about the person who obeys the command.

Right things can be done by right methods for wrong reasons and by the wrong persons. Of uppermost importance is doing all things for Christ's sake. It is to please God that we must do what we do; not because we feel like it, or because of the benefits that we will receive. If there is no stronger motive than feelings, we will not do many things that God requires of us. Christ went to the cross to please God and to save us, despite feelings—strong feelings—to the contrary.

---

1.   The word used in verse 4 means simply to "make wise about" or "to advise." It allows for a variety of ways and means of doing so.

That means that at times we must devise ways and means for doing things that we don't really feel like doing. We will do so because God told us to. That will make it a challenge to implement the commandment. But, often, in the process of developing the implementation of the command you will find that your feelings are already beginning to change so that when you actually put the plan into effect you have more heart for what you will have to do than you did beforehand. If you procrastinate, however, you will not get off square one. Or you will do what you do halfheartedly rather than "heartily." That is one reason Abraham got up "early" the "next morning" (Gen. 22:3, Berkeley) after God told him to sacrifice his only son, Isaac, whom he dearly loved. The implementation of the command had been partially given by God: what was to be done, how it was to be done and where it was to be done were all spelled out (v. 2). But *when* it was to be done was not. Certainly, Abraham did not feel like doing what God commanded. Yet, above all else—even above his son and his own feelings—Abraham wanted to please God by obeying Him. So Abraham determined to do the difficult deed as soon as possible. He may have known that, like so many of us, if he put it off—even till later in the day—he would never do it. In this passage, incidentally, we see linked together, biblically directed and biblically derived implementation. Often, that is the case.

So, frequently, as in the example of Abraham, God allows Christians to become involved in one or more aspects of implementation for their own growth. Abraham was a stronger person for the test of his faith that this event provided (cf. Gen. 22:1). And, as a part of the testing, God left the timing of the event to Abraham's own judgment.

So much more could be said about implementation in general that a book might be written on the subject alone. However, for our present purposes we must move swiftly along to the next consideration.

12

PLANNING

Someone has said, "God plans His work then works His plan." Prophecy is a clear indication that what happens in history is directed, that it has meaning and purpose. History is goal-oriented and what occurs does so in order to bring about certain predetermined ends. In other words, God planned His work and ever since has been working His plan. It is not necessary to list or to discuss the many biblical passages that teach this comforting truth.

Man, who was created in God's image, cannot get along well without planning. That is true in general, but it is especially true of the implementation of biblical teaching in life. Without a plan for putting truth into effect, in many cases the goal will never be realized.

It is important, therefore, for every Christian to recognize the vital nature of planning and to learn how to plan well. Indeed, planning is not just a good idea, it is essential. God *commands* you to plan the implementation of truth in your life. Consider the following two verses:

> ...plan ahead to do what is fine in the eyes of everyone (Rom. 12:17).

> ...put on the Lord Jesus Christ and don't make plans to satisfy the desires of the flesh (Rom. 13:14).

The same Greek word, *pronoeo,* is used in both of those verses. It means to make arrangements and provision ahead of time for something that is to be done, i.e., to plan and prepare.

It is especially interesting to note that God must warn us not to plan to do wrong things. Man is a creature who is like God and who, therefore, plans. He cannot help planning; he is an incurable planner by nature. It is not a matter of planning or not planning; if he will not plan ahead "to do what is fine," you can be sure that he will be busy planning to "satisfy the desires of the flesh"!

But notice carefully: in order to achieve what is fine (*kalos* is the Greek term used; it means more than what is morally good [*agathos*]. It speaks of the quality of the action itself, intrinsically and as it is perceived by others); one must "make arrangements" and "make provision" for that result. It will not come off well without careful forethought and action. In other words, planning takes time, thought, and effort to produce "fine" results. Nothing truly fine ever happens without planning, whether it is a fine meal or a fine wedding, fine music or preaching in a worship service. That is what God requires of us—*fine* action, action with finesse.

Whatever God's people do, they must do it first for Him; there should be no wonder, then, that they do *fine* things. What less is worthy of Him? But it is because they work for him that they continue to put out the extra thought and effort to do something in a fine way, even when no one else appreciates it. The Christian knows that when others misunderstand, criticize or ignore their efforts, it is "the Lord Christ" whom they serve (Col. 3:24). They work for the boss only incidentally. They do not need his compliments and encouragement to do a fine job; it is enough to know that some day Christ will say "well done." That keeps them putting out that extra effort to be sure that whatever they do is fine. But, as a matter of fact, serving Christ means that they will serve the boss or the company better; the two are complementary, not antithetical. Working for Christ produces the finest work for the boss.

So, in implementing the truth learned, it is necessary to do adequate planning whenever it is possible to do so. Much of that planning comes through meditation on the Scriptures prior to doing what must be done. Whenever one studies the Bible *telically*, concerned about what the Holy Spirit has in mind for later retrieval, he will begin immediately to reflect on the life-changing import of the truths learned. He will want to figure out ways and means of translating those truths into life and ministry as soon as possible. In order to do so, he should make it a practice to ask:

1. How must my life change to conform to what I have just learned?
2. How can I begin to minister this truth to others?

If he keeps those two questions in mind when studying the Scriptures and faithfully answers them with his life (not only with his mind), he will be neither unfruitful nor useless.

Indeed, life alteration should be so much a part of his daily study itself that as he interprets he begins to jot down ways and means for achieving the ends that God has set forth in the Bible. But, though he should always be concerned about answering the two questions above, he must do so *in the order given*—starting with change in his own life.

When one begins to *use* the Scriptures that he interprets in his daily study, he will find that he is developing a framework, a set of procedures, as well as a mind-set, for meeting Thursday's emergencies. And, day by day, he will be building a stockpile of information and methods for doing so. New contingencies can be related to the framework that he will be erecting daily.

Let's take an example. Mary has been studying the latter part of Romans 12, the passage from which that verse about planning ahead comes. Among other things, she reads, "Bless those who persecute you." That strikes her hard. She isn't doing that; in fact, she doesn't even know how! She learns further that this is one way to *overcome evil* with good (v. 21). And as she studies the word "bless" in Vine, etc., she discovers that it is the Greek term from which our English word "eulogize" comes. Somehow, she is to eulogize (speak well of and beneficially to) those who persecute her. Rather than return words in kind, she must "bless" and curse not (12:14[b]). Clearly, this is going to take repentance, thought, and planning as well as practice. She asks, "Who are my persecutors?" and immediately thinks of several women at work who seem to derive a particular pleasure from making catty, cutting remarks about her and her faith. True, when compared with what the martyrs endured, hers is a minor sort of persecution, but it has been growing heavy lately, and Mary knows that she has not handled it well so far. And, anyway, it is *her* persecution—the only one that she has—and she must grapple with it. If she can't handle this, how could she ever handle something really severe? Now, through her Bible study, she has found God's way of doing so. It is time for a counterattack—of love!

God wants Mary to plan, to take the time to think ahead and to think hard about ways to speak well of these women to others, and to speak kindly to them in response to their cutting comments. That will not be easy; it will take some thought, attitude change, and discipline. He wants her to be prepared for anything they may do or say. And she must be prepared to make a *fine* response.

Mary will have to plan. She will have to recall some of the unpleasant remarks of the past and how she responded. It won't be very nice to resurrect these, but she will need to use them as paradigms for future encounters. She must not recall them in order to keep the issue alive, or to dwell on them in any spirit of bitterness, but for the following reasons.

1. By examining the sort of thing that has been going on, she will look for patterns: does it always occur at a certain time? Or does it usually take place at a particular location? Or, perhaps, is it connected with certain subjects? Or what? If there is a

discernible pattern (or two), that will help her to watch out for the occasions connected with it, and to prepare more concretely for those issues, etc., over which it may arise.

2. She must recall unpleasant remarks to examine her own past responses. Was she ever successful in answering as Christ would have answered? If so, how? Exactly what made that a success? This insight may help her to pattern future responses along similar lines. How did she fail? One way? Several ways? Noting these ways, she may prayerfully ask God to help her avoid such failure in the future. And that is the prelude to the next step.

3. Reviewing past remarks will help Mary to develop new biblical ways of responding in the future. This implementation is necessary since the Bible doesn't tell her precisely *how* to do so. By going back over specific failures in the past, she may ask, "How should I have responded?" Then, she may develop better ways of meeting those situations—replies that would be a success in God's sight. This will afford her practice and will enable her to gain confidence as she goes to work and faces these women again. She will be aware of the sort of thing that they have been saying, and she will now be armed with the sort of blessings that she ought to be returning in reply.

4. Mary should not merely wait to respond, however; she should take the offensive and begin to do good for those who persecute her. This too will have to be planned in order to be executed with finesse. But even the realization that she is not simply a sitting duck for others to take pot shots at, but rather, that she can take the situation into hand and begin to develop it in ways that please God (by His help, of course), is itself an exciting fact. The women are not in control; by the grace of God, she is. She has declared war on them; and she is out to overcome their evil with good. If at all possible, she will take them captive for Christ.

That is the way that the study of a portion of the Scriptures should affect a student of the Bible. It should change things. No passage studied, interpreted correctly and applied to one's situation should ever be put on the shelf and left there to rot; it should be implemented immediately—turned into fruit!

These efforts, planned, perhaps even worked out on paper, and becoming a part of a regular prayer list, take time and preparation to be pulled off well. It will take time to think of good things to say about Mary's persecutors. Mary must be careful not to be hypocritical in what she does and says. She must be truthful; she may not flatter. She must search for things that she may honestly commend. When we do not think biblically, our minds focus on and often magnify the evil in another. We may even begin to see evil where it does not exist. It will take prayerful meditation (please see *Ready to Restore* on this: meditation probably is not what you think it is) just to begin to approach the whole matter as a Christian should.

So often we strike back in a manner that Romans 12:14[b] forbids. Mary must take time to discover, repent of, and overcome past patterns. As she meditates about such matters, she will recognize that there is much to be done if she is to respond finely. She may find it necessary to lay aside all other Bible study for a week or two while she develops all of the other passages related to Romans 14, so that she can meet the situation with a full understanding of what she must do. There is no need to read a certain number of arbitrarily chosen verses a day. Better to sit down hard on a passage, or six, until that truth has been thoroughly digested and kneaded into the dough of your life.

It is just such a study and struggle that prepares. Without both, Mary, or any of the rest of us, is sure to fail God. A successful medical operation is the result of many hours, days and weeks of personal preparation in learning theory, techniques and skills. So too, in a greater sense, we struggle with the Scriptures, wrestling until they touch our thigh. And as we come to grips with the meaning of a passage for our lives, we must never let it go until it blesses us!

So, what I am saying is this: Mary will know what to do on Thursday because she has agonized over it on Wednesday, and Tuesday, and Monday too. She has readied herself before God and for others so that on Thursday, though she has no idea what will be said or when, if at all, she will be as ready as possible for every contingency. There will be much from Romans 14 and from parallel passages that will be stored up in her heart. She will go to work with the Word of Christ "dwelling richly" within her. It will not merely be a matter of memorized Bible verses, but a matter of a prepared person.

When she is thus prepared, instead of cringing fear that at times made her want to stay home from work, she will now go enthusiastically, hopeful that some word spoken may be used by God to subdue hard hearts. Fear and embarrassment will be replaced by a new sense of holy boldness and confidence. This is noticeable to others (Acts 4:13), and once again in her life may point beyond her to Jesus, as it did in the account in Acts.

So, as in every effort that is done well, planning is essential to handling problems on Thursday.

But one note of caution. Human planning is not the same as divine planning. No matter how good they look on Wednesday, we must not think that our plans are the law of the Medes and the Persians—unchangeable and absolute. They may have to be modified on Thursday. Indeed, part of good human planning is to prepare for possible change.

We cannot anticipate all contingencies. We do not know exactly what will happen on Thursday. We do not know what *God* is planning to do. So after planning well, we should submit our best plans to God for His blue-penciling. Then, when it comes, we must rejoice in it. That is what James is getting at in 4:13-16. He does not forbid planning; no, exactly the opposite. What he forbids is canned-and-refrigerated planning. He teaches flexible planning; conditional planning. We must write across every page of planning, "If the Lord wills." for a while, at least, you might literally do so (by the way, *writing out* plans keeps you from fuzzy thinking and also serves as a reminder), using, perhaps, the well-known *D.V.* abbreviation (*Deo volente:* "Lord willing").

All of which leads to the next chapter.

13

GOAL SETTING AND SCHEDULING

Above all other goals for the Christian is one: pleasing God. Indeed, this one goal is the foundation for adopting and for implementing any goal in life; whether it is a long-term goal or a short-term goal. If something I might do pleases God, I should make it my goal to do it; if it does not, I must remove or reject it as a goal. As Paul put it: "...we make it our ambition to please Him" (II Cor. 5:9).

The English word "implementation" has a root that means "to fill up." An implement is an article, instrument, tool or piece of equipment that is used in the process of filling up (fulfilling) some goal. The word refers to carrying out an objective so as to give practical effect to a purpose by means of concrete measures. Implementation, then, has to do with goals and objectives and may apply to whatever one finds it necessary to do to effect an end.

GOAL SETTING

Whether one speaks of "goals" or "objectives" or "ends" to me is immaterial. From reading much literature in which these words are used, I can hardly fail to note that though they are often distinguished, there is little consistency among English-speaking writers about how they ought to be distinguished. In my own usage, they are almost entirely synonymous, with "objective" and "end," perhaps, getting the edge over "goal" when I speak of what is long range, and "goal" more frequently used for what is closer at hand. But, on the other hand, I feel equally comfortable in speaking of short-term and long-term goals. Short-term goals are the mileposts you must pass to reach longer-term goals; they are often necessary steps that must be taken to get there. In this chapter, to avoid any confusion, I will largely confine myself to the use of the words short-term and long-term goals.

What ever terminology you use, you must distinguish between short- and long-term goals. Some goals are close at hand, and actually are stepping stones across the brook that enable you to get to the more distant goals that lie on the other bank. New Testament writers everywhere recognize this distinction. They think and they write in terms of it. Consider a few typical examples from the pen of the apostle Peter:

> ... Christ Himself suffered in your place, leaving behind a pattern for you to copy *so that* you might follow in His steps (I Pet. 2:21).

The pattern (outlined in vv. 22, 23) is given for us to "copy" (our near or proximate goal) so that we might "follow in His steps," or live like Him (our long-range goal). Consider another in I Peter 3:1:

> ...wives, submit to your husbands [the short-term goal] *so that* even if some of them disobey the Word, they may be won without a word by the behavior of their wives [the long-term goal].

And, of course, the ultimate goal (no other goal is ultimate) behind all others also frequently comes to the fore:

> When someone speaks, let him speak God's messages; when someone serves, let him serve by the strength that God supplies, *so that* in everything God may be glorified through Jesus Christ, to Whom be glory and might forever and ever. Amen (I Pet. 4:11).

That goal, though not explicitly mentioned in the two quotations given before, in Peter's thinking, nevertheless, lay behind all that he wrote. And it should always do so in all of our thinking too. Some purists want a statement of the ultimate goal always to accompany statements of other goals, just as some always attach *D.V.* to every statement about planning. This is demanding too much because it amounts to demanding more of us than the Bible does, and implicitly condemns the Bible's own practice of sometimes mentioning it and sometimes not doing so. It is dangerous to be more pious than Peter.

However, the ultimate goal always must be part of all goal setting, even if not expressed in words. If a wife alters her behavior *first* to please God in obedience to Him, for His glory, and only *secondly* in order to win her husband, even if that husband is never saved (there is no absolute promise that he will be), she will always be successful in achieving her primary goal. Thus, when his goals are right, a Christian has the assurance that it is always possible to realize his ultimate goal. And the wife will not stop living as she should because it has not had the desired effect on her husband (i.e., her second goal has not been reached), but she will go on living as she should because she did not make the changes as a gimmick to get her way about her husband; she changed, basically, in order to please God.

Now, we speak of working toward goals. All human motivation is goal oriented. When we eat, drink, buy, sell, go to bed, get up, pray, complain, we do all of these things in order to attain certain ends. These ends may be known, unknown, or partially known to us; they may be simple or complex. The goals may be well thought through or poorly chosen; they may be helpful goals or harmful. They may be Christian or pagan. But, nonetheless, whatever we do in life is goal oriented.

A Christian's goals may grow out of clearly defined, accepted and articulated philosophies based on well-understood biblical presuppositions. But it is a rare case in which that is so.

Normally, like the world, Christians drift with the prevailing currents of thought and action. Most unbelievers do this all of the time. There are, of course, exceptions to this rule. Here and there you will find persons who are not following the crowd (or some particular crowd); they are leading it. They are persons with precisely laid plans. Others react; they do not act. They allow themselves to become pawns in the hands of the goal-oriented persons around them. They drift into habitual routines which, although they do not consciously choose most of them, they allow to chart and control their earthly, and often, their eternal destinies.

Christians must follow neither crowds nor feelings; they need neither drift nor randomly adopt habit patterns. Unfortunately, many do. They must become actors, not *reactors*.

They must learn to choose and develop goals, structure their lives and become actors who consciously do whatever they do in order to attain biblical goals. These goals—even the short-term goals—must be biblical. They must "seek first the kingdom of God and His righteousness," not the by-products ("all these things"), that the world puts first.

All of these goals ought to be plainly known. At first, at least, it is best to try to sketch them out on paper. Otherwise, it is possible to deceive one's self into thinking that he knows what his life goals are when he doesn't. Can you sit down right now and do so? I challenge you. Do it, at least in a broad, general way. Why not give it a try in the following space? Write in pencil.

Ultimate Goal: To Glorify God

By...	By...
List at least 10 long-term goals	Next to each long-term goal list at least three short-term goals that will help you attain it
1.	A. B. C.
2.	A. B. C.

3.	A.
	B.
	C.
4.	A.
	B.
	C.
5.	A.
	B.
	C.
6.	A.
	B.
	C.

7.

A.

B.

C.

8.

A.

B.

C.

9.

A.

B.

C.

10.

A.

B.

C.

Now, having listed your 10 goals, arrange them below in order of priority:

1.

2.

3.

4.

5.

6.

7.

8.

9.

10.

Keep these goals before you. Transfer them into a larger (or longer) book in time, writing always in pencil and allowing more space for additional material.

I suggest that you write in pencil because (1) you may refine, restate and revise your goals from time to time as your biblical understanding of your life and ministry grows, and (2) you may be able to add to the list the results of your regular studies in the Bible.

The framing of such a growing, flexible goal structure for your life will greatly facilitate your decision making on Thursday. You will find that you are continually able to plug new truth into the context of your life and ministry because you will have a framework into which it may be fitted. The structure will help you to keep priorities straight, and will remind you to consider the place of daily decisions in your overall plans.

If a given action furthers your plans in some biblical way, it ought to be taken; if it does not—even though good in itself—it is likely that it ought to be rejected. I assume here that the overall plan is biblically correct.

However, one way to decide when planning must be revised is to consider the clash of a new future good option with one's present plans and priorities. Sometimes God sends options to challenge and upset our planning ("This opens a new avenue that I had never considered before"), sometimes to test us to see if we will stick to good planning ("Ah, but that would move me off God's track"), and sometimes to help us refine and to clarify our planning ("I wonder what the impact of this would be on...").

However you look at it, you *will* have goals and you *will* live according to them. So it is most important to choose your goals carefully, consciously and correctly from a biblical perspective.

SCHEDULING

No matter how good your goals may be, without a schedule by which you may determine when you must attain those goals, you will find that your efforts at goal setting will be fruitless. Many good intentions and many well-chosen courses of action have foundered exactly at this point.

God is a goal setting and a schedule making God. Prophecy is pre-recorded history. The coming of Christ was according to schedule (Gal. 4:4). If God schedules and operates according to schedule, who are we to think that we can avoid doing so?

A few words concerning this important matter may be helpful. God himself works according to schedule. The *plan* of redemption included a timetable. Christ came "in the fullness of time" (Gal. 4:4); His death was predicted to the half year (Dan.

9:20-27, esp. vv. 26, 27); He Himself declared, "My time is not yet at hand" (John 7:6) and often spoke of the "hour" of (appointed time for) His death (John 12:27; 17:1, etc.). If God is orderly in His workings, and you were created in His image, how do you think that you can succeed by being disorderly?

A typical scheduling assignment might read as follows: "Develop a weekly schedule in which the various essential (i.e., demanded by God's Word) elements of your life are placed on the schedule, with adequate time provided for all that God requires of you." Remember, God says that you are to do all your work in six days. But remember also that all of your work includes work of different sorts; e.g., you need to distinguish between your employment and the odd jobs around the house.[1] The six days include both. You must find time for doing your work at home. When you do, many of the problems between you and your wife may cease. This sort of work is every bit as important as the labor for which you are paid.

Sometimes Christians identify scheduling with adding tasks. However, scheduling may involve eliminating matters of lesser importance that get in the way of essentials. Perhaps honest scheduling will show that time for lower priority items can be found only occasionally but not regularly. Some meeting, for instance, may have to be cancelled in order to find time for the family.[2] God's priorities never conflict. Conflict and confusion stem from sin, not from God.

Those who excuse themselves by saying that they have no time to do what God commands need to be told that they *do* have

---

1. Fixing doors or sleds, cutting the grass, hanging wallpaper, repairing doll furniture, etc., playing with children, legitimately is part of the six-day work. Those who work six days at their employment may need to revise their schedules or even change their jobs in order to do *"all* their work" (Ex. 20:9).

2. The family should not be torn apart by church meetings. Many meetings are important for particular persons; we should not necessarily seek crowds at these meetings, but urge *only those who need* this meeting to attend.

the time: "We all have the same size pie—twenty-four hours each day. Everything depends upon how you slice it."

The record of what you actually do with your time that you may keep over a three-day to one-week period[1] should be analyzed not only for time leakage, but also should be compared with what you ought to be doing. Then immediate adjustments (put it off and you may never get to it) must be made to bring the real into correspondence with ideal. Sometimes this must be done by phasing out and phasing in. Obligations and responsibilities cannot all be dropped at once. But more frequently the needed changes will require immediate, stiffer, more decisive action (e.g., phoning the Little League office and resigning as leader effective in a month).

At all costs, persons with problems of scheduling must come to the place where they draw up what they believe before God to be a righteous schedule that honors Him by providing adequate and balanced time for all of those life priorities required in the Scriptures.[2]

Balance in one's use of time is achieved not merely by *quantitative* adjustments; *quality* is crucial also. Two hours of quality time (rather than mere togetherness) with one's wife or child may be worth two days of other activities with them.

Therefore, consider scheduling balances in terms of *how much?* But also in terms of *what kind?* What one does can be of much greater significance than how long he does it. A heart-to-heart talk about a problem that lasts thirty minutes could cement a relationship for a lifetime. Five words taking less than one minute can destroy a marriage. As one joke puts it: "Too much

---

1.   What my counseling associate, George Scipione, calls a "portable schedule." A small spiral notebook carried in pocket or purse is probably most useful.

2.   Including such factors as time for spouse, prayer, church, witnessing, family, work, personal cultivation, sleep, exercise, fellowship, etc. Be sure to build in fudge factors for emergencies. Leisure time, relaxation, and rest are essential. Passivities as well as activities should be included.

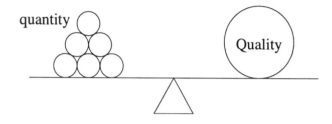

togetherness is tearing us apart." The point of the joke for a Christian is, of course, that counterproductive togetherness exposes the lack of a quality relationship in Christ.

Flexibility

Scheduling, contrary to what many think, is the only road to flexibility; organization is the only way to freedom. The disorganized, unscheduled person never knows, for instance, when to say yes or no. He is not free to assume a new obligation or to relinquish an old one without confusion and guilt. Since he does not know how much time is needed to do what he has already obligated himself to, he is *bound* by his ignorance. He cannot freely switch or substitute obligations as situations change, since without planning he does not know what may be swapped with what. In short, the failure to take the time to plan, arrange, organize, and schedule makes one fearful, guilty and inflexible.

Since many problems come from failing to carry on one's affairs decently and in order, it is frequently essential to learn how to become orderly and how to schedule your life. You cannot avoid the matter. God is not a God of confusion (I Cor. 14:33): it is such sins as jealously and selfish ambition[1] that lead

---

1. Pastors and Christian workers who over-schedule their lives often do so out of pride and ambition. Yet nothing less than confusion of life is the result. Sleep is a vital essential that should be scheduled first. Eight hours, scheduled regularly, should be the

to disorder, as well as every other sort of evil (James 3:16). Disorderly housewives, husbands who have never learned to say "no" to demands upon their time, guilty Christian workers who never seem to complete projects, and persons who fail to keep appointments and meet basic life responsibilities all have one thing in common—they are living in a disorganized and confused way. Whatever the difficulties that may have led to disorderliness, the pattern itself must be met and handled as a separate problem.[1]

PLANNING AND SCHEDULING

Sometimes it is wise for you to begin by keeping a record of how you now spend your time. For a week, in a small notebook that can be carried in the pocket, note briefly the exact time and the activity (or nonactivity) every time that a change is made. You may discover with many others that hours are being nickeled and dimed away in bits and pieces. Combined, a wasted 15 minutes here, 20 minutes there, and a half hour at a third point could provide significant blocks of additional time for important projects that are now being neglected. Moreover, study of the record may indicate foolish, wasteful patterns of activity in which, for example, travel (visitation, perhaps) patterns show unnecessary duplications that might be eliminated at great savings of both gasoline and time.

But when it becomes clear that something must be done to change the situation, what should you do? First, recognize the great importance of drawing up a schedule: God Himself works by a schedule.[2] The adjustments in present patterns must be

---

consistent practice of every counselor and counselee if he wishes to act efficiently and not sin against his body, which for the Christian is the temple of the Holy Spirit. A good bed is a good investment; one-third of one's life is spent in it!

1.   Jay E. Adams, *The Christian Counselor's* Manual (Grand Rapids, MI; Zondervan, 1973), pp. 338-42.

2.   Cf. ibid., p. 173.

made according to biblical priorities. Making a list as follows
may help.[1]

Worksheet for Scheduling

Unprofitable Activities to discontinue	Profitable Activities to continue or add	Items from Column Two in order of priority

---

1.   Jay. E. Adams, *Shepherding God's Flock* (Grand Rapids, MI, Zondervan, 1980), pp. 41-42.

STICKING TO THE SCHEDULE

Schedules should be considered servants, not masters. That means that, unlike the laws of the Medes and Persians, they must be made to allow for change and alteration. But this change should involve largely *shifts* in elements that already have been scheduled, or the use of time allotted for emergencies, opportunities, etc. Only rarely should change mean that good plans should be altered. If the original plans are good, proper in the sight of God, and the contemplated change cannot be brought about by the existing flexibility that the schedule provides, question seriously whether the change ought to be made. Such changes, in the long run, are rarely opportunities. On the other hand, when the contemplated change *genuinely* seems to demand an alteration in the schedule, at least two things should happen: (1) The schedule should be apprised to see if the change has not exposed flaws in the schedule that must be removed. There should follow a prayerful revision of the schedule leading toward improvement.[1] (2) If the contemplated change does not require permanent change, consideration must be given to *what* may be changed *when,* and for *how long.* You will find that there is an irreducible number of top priority items that cannot be changed.[2] These must be known and identified *before* the pressure to change occurs. Otherwise, it will be too easy to allow for wrong changes to be made.

---

1. From time to time one's schedule should be reviewed; situations change. Health problems, for example, may demand alteration. If on review a pastor sees that he has taken on too much, he should not hesitate to cancel meetings, resign from committees or groups, or whatever is necessary to assume his proper obligations before God. Fatigue, strains and stress at home, excessive tension, etc., all may be signs pointing toward the review of one's schedule. Some specific items, of course, will be filled in at the appropriate places each week; others each morning. Flexibility to alter one's schedule according to God's providence must always be maintained; scheduling must never violate the principles of James 4:13-17.

2. Such as personal Bible study and prayer, time with wife and children, etc.

If, for example, you are invited to attend a meeting that is not an absolute necessity, and upon looking at your appointment book you notice you have marked that hour off for time to spend with the children, unless you can find an equally good time to which you can move the family outing, decline the invitation, saying, "I'm sorry, I have an important obligation already scheduled for that time." That is not a lie; it is the truth. One's obligations to his family must be of the *utmost* importance.

So, from all this you can see something of the importance of making and keeping schedules. May I suggest that you rough in a time for every short-term goal in your program as well as for some of the long-term goals? Again, these may have to be revised or adjusted, they ought to be realistic, and they must be entirely subject to God's timing. But if there is nothing to revise, you will always be confused, bound by chaos and uncertainty. Learn the joy not only of discovering truth, but of planning and actually putting it into practice. A significant element in any successful implementation of one's Bible study will be good scheduling.

14

ADAPTATION

When I speak of adaptation, I am not referring to the revisions and refinements that you must make in the goal oriented life structure that we have just been discussing in the previous chapter. Of course, adaptation—adjusting one thing to fit another[1]—occurs throughout that process too. But that is not in view here.

What I have in mind is this: in order to be useful, truth in the Bible must be adapted to similar though not identical situations in our lives today. Many persons falter at just this point. Either they do not see the identity between the biblical passage and their life situation, or they make invalid and improper identifications that will, as a result, lead them astray. It is identity and difference with which we must learn to deal in adaptation.

When I spoke about telic analysis earlier in this book, I was laying the foundation for both the proper understanding and the adaptation of Scripture to daily life. Much of the uncertainty experienced on Thursday arises from not knowing how to adapt the Bible to modern situations.

Fundamentally, as I have suggested, there are two factors involved in all adaptation: identities and differences. We shall consider each separately.

IDENTITY

In seeking to understand the telic thrust of a passage, one is attempting to discover the Holy Spirit's purpose or intent. "What does he want to do to me, my church, etc.?" is the question

1. The word "adapt" means, literally, "to fit to."

before you. When you can answer that question accurately, you will be well on your way to adapting the truth to the present day situation that is under consideration. In order to answer that question clearly, you must know how to abstract the principle in a passage.

To abstract a scriptural principle requires understanding and practice. In order to abstract a telic principle you must be able to ask and answer these questions:

1. What is the general purpose of the passage:
   a. to inform?
   b. to convince?
   c. to motivate

2. What is the specific purpose of the passage:
   a. to inform me about what?
   b. to convince me to believe or disbelieve what?
   c. to motivate me to do or to cease doing what?

Whenever you can answer those questions, you will be able to state the telic thrust of the passage in one simple sense: In this passage, the Holy Spirit intends to __(state general purpose)__ me to __(state specific purpose)__.

At first, and for a long time to come, as the upshot of every Bible study, I suggest that you actually write out such a statement, in the format just given, filling in the blanks according to the teaching of each passage. Force yourself to state the telic thrust.

Because I Corinthians 10:13[1] is true, we know that God's solutions to basic problems in ancient Israel were applicable to the situations in Corinth, even though many Corinthians might have thought that they were not because they lived at a much later time in history. "Times have changed so much," some must

---

1.   "No trial has taken hold of you except that which other people have experienced; but God is faithful Who will not allow you to be tried beyond what you are able to bear, but rather, will provide together with the trial the way out so that you may be able to endure it.."

have thought. The same objections, of course, are raised today: "How can words written to Israelites, or to Corinthians for that matter, have much relevance to persons who are living at this late date in history?" Like the Corinthians, they see widely differing forms of circumstances and tend to say, "How can that apply to me?"

But Paul is clear:

> Now these events happened as examples for *us*...these events happened to them as examples that were recorded as counsel for *us* who live at this late date in history (I Cor. 10:6, 10).

The words translated "examples" are *tupos* and *tupikos,* which mean "example" or "pattern" and "by way of example." These terms make it clear that the principles that may be abstracted from the events can be a pattern for any age. The reason is given in I Corinthians 10:13; "No trial has taken hold of you except that which other people have experienced." There is an identity to human problems and experiences in all ages. It is our task in adapting biblical truth to our times and to our situation to discover those basic identities so that we shall know what is (and what is not) now applicable.

That which is identical, and thus applicable to any age, is that which may be abstracted as a principle stated in the form of a telic proposition such as I have described above.

DIFFERENCE

Adaptation is necessary because of differences, not because of identities. The identities are what make it possible. But because of the differences, which otherwise can get in the way, the identities must be made to fit by translating them into the terms and forms of new ones. Differences can cloud one's perception of identities if he does not know how to look past them to identities. The telic, abstracting process is what weeds out the identities from the maze of differences in which they are embedded.

Now the adaptation process consists of three steps:
1. Identifying identities (this is done through the procedures used to identify the telic thrust of a passage);
2. Abstracting identities in a telic statement;
3. Reintroducing the identity into the milieu of new circumstances in a new era.

These differences are not basic, as we have seen from I Corinthians 10:13 (for a full discussion of the verse, see my pamphlet, *Christ and Your Problems* [Phillipsburg, N.J.: Presbyterian and Reformed, 1971]). Yet they are nonetheless important. If the identity is not properly reintroduced into the new milieu, there will be no adaptation, but either an *accommodation* of truth (in which the identity is bent, twisted, covered over or otherwise mutilated and distorted to fit the new situation) or an *agglomeration* (in which an identity is unnaturally mixed with, but not fitted to, the new milieu in such a way that it appears totally inappropriate and inapplicable). In true adaptation, identities and differences are both fitted in new and creative ways, preserving the context intact while redressing it in contemporary garb that blends rather than clashes with the modern milieu.

Let's consider some examples that will help make these issues plain. In them, we shall see accommodation, agglomeration and adaptation at work.

In a recently published book we read,

> It seems so difficult to bring people to believe that *they* can hear God's voice. Members of the Church of the Savior in Washington, D.C., have been experimenting in this field for some time. Their conclusion: "We think that we are twentieth and twenty-first century people; nonetheless, we have hints that one can receive directions as clear as those given

Annanias... 'Rise and go to the street called straight.'"[1]

The writer of the book then asks, "Why not?" The answer, of course, lies in the fact that although in Acts 9:10, 11 there is a record of God speaking in direct revelation today, the Holy Spirit's intention in that passage is not to teach us to seek direct revelation today. A careful telic analysis of the passage would reveal quite a different telic thrust. The people at the Church of the Savior, I am afraid, receive their "hints" not as the result of historical-grammatical-rhetorical-theological exegesis (interpretation), leading to a telic understanding of what the Spirit intended to do for them in the historical narrative in Acts, to which they refer, but from their extra-biblical "experimentation." In order to reach the "conclusions" at which they arrived, they had to ignore true differences between first century, apostolic, non-revelatory ones and modern ones. They relate them *as if* the differences were *intended* identities. Telic analysis of the passage will show that the Holy Spirit had no intention of teaching either the first reader of Acts, or any others who would read it in subsequent times, that we could, or should, receive direct revelation through meditation, as Foster supposes. His true purpose in the narrative was to inform us about the background of and the conversion of Paul, who, in the outworking of God's program of evangelism outlined in Acts 1:8, would be the principal one to carry the witness to the Gentile world and eventually to Rome. There is no indication whatever of any telic intent to instruct us in the ways and means of obtaining direct revelation. The passage has no emphasis on meditation at all.

In that erroneous understanding and use of Acts 9 we encounter an all too typical instance of accommodation. The biblical passage has been distorted to meet a modern situation. It

---

1.   Richard J. Foster, *Celebration of discipline* (New York: Harper and Row, 1978), p. 19.

has been used to answer questions that Luke never intended anyone to ask of it. Accommodation by misuse has occurred so that rather than being used, in power, by matching true identities in the biblical and current milieus, the passage has been weakened. It has been used for the writer's purpose, not for the purpose for which it was intended. One of these might be to demonstrate how God can subdue His enemies. Another might be to teach that God's program will be carried out regardless of man's opposition. There are others. But look at this for a moment:

The teaching abstracted in telic terms ("in this passage, God intended to inform the reader that His program will be carried out regardless of man's opposition") becomes immediately adaptable to modern situations. The abstracting process divests the truth of all the time-cultural and particularized features that comprise the differences. Thus, they are as ready to fit all relevant situations as the modern socks that are advertized, "One size fits all."

Note well, however, any abstracting—even the wrong one (e.g., "In this passage God intended to motivate us to seek direct revelation through meditation")—is immediately adaptable. Thus, the criterion for correctness in adaptation is not ease of adaptation, but correctness in properly locating and identifying the telic thrusts of any given passage.

Now let's take another example. Agglomeration occurs when one attempts to put two or more unlike situations (those containing no telic identities) together. When they are agglomerated, each retains its own separate and distinct identity and sticks out from the others in an unnatural and forced bond. No adaptation takes place because there can be no fit. Listen to the following:

> When Iran was about to fall, a portion of our fleet travelled into the Indian Ocean. Our President was told if he wanted SALT II to be successful, he should remove those ships immediately. The ships were

removed. Where is our moral courage? Where are those who will stand for right? The Lord said, "Have not I commanded thee? Be strong and of good courage; be not afraid, neither be thou dismayed; for the Lord thy God is with thee wherever thou goest."[1]

I happen to agree that we have often lacked moral courage as a nation, that trust in God alone can provide such courage, and even that we should not have removed our ships. However, the passage of Scripture used to substantiate the author's viewpoint in fact does not do so; the two (the passage and the modern situation) have been agglomerated. The matter at issue was removal of the fleet. But does removal of the fleet really prove lack of courage? Possibly. Possibly not. There may be a great deal more behind the action than one can discover through the news media. Perhaps it was merely strategy (bad, perhaps; perhaps good, for all we know of what is really going on behind the scenes). Secondly, as the passage indicates, Joshua had *God's direct command to carry out a divinely revealed program.* It was a Program in which he would face many dangers and much opposition, and there would be occasions for discouragement; he would therefore need strength, hope and courage to carry it out. But there was no divine program from which President Carter veered when he took his action. Nor did he have a divine command to keep the ships there. The two situations differ greatly—so greatly that to put them together is to agglomerate them, not to adapt them.

If, however, in the pursuit of some endeavor that God has commanded in the Scriptures (let us say attempting to preach the gospel in a ghetto) one is exposed to danger, opposition, discouragement, etc., the passage might be applied readily. Adaptation would take place easily.

The misuse of Scripture is so common that it was simple to pick up two books at random that happened to be lying on my

---

1.   Charles F. Stanley, *Stand Up America* (Atlanta: In Touch Ministries, 1980).

desk and, with little or no trouble, to discover in one an instance of accommodation and in the other an instance of agglomeration.

Accommodation can take place in a number of ways. But when, because of misinterpretation or misapplication, a passage is made to fit a situation that it doesn't really fit, that, in essence, is the dynamic behind all accommodation: the Scriptures are accommodated to purposes of the one misusing them. This can occur through ignorance, lack of care, or for other reasons, but regardless of the cause, the result is the same. The problem is not a new one (cf. II Pet. 3:16).

Agglomeration also entails a misinterpretation of the Bible, but in doing so the Bible is not so much bent out of shape (as in accommodation) as it is misapplied.

What changes in adaptation is not the telic thrust, but the incidental circumstances. In the parable of the good Samaritan, there are many features that must be altered to bring it up to date in order to apply it personally. There won't be any priests or Levites around to work with, and the Samaritan will not be found on a road to Jericho. But respected religious leaders will be around in bucketfuls, and the problem of their lack of compassionate neighborliness will make its appearance. Instead of Samaritans, the ethnic and religious half-breeds that the Jews despised, any number of persons might be substituted, depending on who it is that in a given community of persons is looked at that way. But, in all of that change, the telic thrust of the passage will remain intact.

So, from this chapter, I hope that you will be alerted to false ways of using the Bible and prepared to check continually what you are doing to make sure that you are properly using the Bible by adapting it rather than doing something else. Attention to this matter over a period of time will make it a part of your regular use of the Scriptures, so that on Thursday, when problems arise, you will handle the Bible rightly and thereby obtain correct solutions to them.

CONCLUSION

You have persisted to the end. Congratulations! You are one of those persons who truly cares about the matter we have been considering. But do you care enough not only to read but to do what must be done to be able to use your Bible in a practical way on Thursday?

It will cost you to do so. You will have to buy some books. You will have to carve out time for serious Bible study and planning. You will have to think and be creative. You will find it necessary to keep records, learn and memorize the locations of principal passages, set goals, make schedules and keep them and live according to priorities. You will have to make life changes too. It will cost!

But the results will be worth the cost; you cannot do all of the things that you are encouraged to do in this book without noticeable results. Think of what it will mean to *really* know and use your Bible at last! Is there any other effort more important than this one? Can you expend so little time (six months) for such a large return doing anything else? Consider carefully what you will do now that you have come to the end of this book.

You have various options. You could lay it aside with all good intentions to return to it some time when you "are not so busy." But let me ask you, when do you think that you are going to have more time than now? You know that those days hardly ever come. Don't kid yourself. Moreover, when do you think that you will be ever be more inclined to begin than right now? No, there is no better time to start than now.

"Now?" Yes, now. "*Right* now?" Yes, if possible, do a good bit; if not, do *something* to break the ice. Set your goals; schedule something else out and schedule in at least a half hour each day to pursue this program. Decide what books you need to buy,

and get (or order) as many of them as you can *today*. Hold your
first study period *today*. Don't wait even until tomorrow, unless
it is now past midnight. In that case, remember Abraham—rise
up early tomorrow, and begin. Make a start! Half the trip is the
first few steps. It will change your life.